THE BILL REED COLLECTION

THE LAST DAYS OF
SCOTTISH STEAM

IN FULL COLOUR

PETER TUFFREY

GREAT N ORTHERN

ACKNOWLEDGEMENTS

I am grateful for help of the following people: David Burrill, Cathryn at Book Law (Nottingham), Barry Cox, David Joy, Hugh Parkin, Bill Reed.

Special thanks to my son Tristram Tuffrey for his general help behind the scenes.

INFORMATION

I have taken reasonable steps to verify the accuracy of the information in this book but it may contain errors or omissions. Any information that may be of assistance to rectify any problems will be gratefully received. Please contact me by email: petertuffrey@rocketmail.com - or in writing: Peter Tuffrey, 8 Wrightson Avenue, Warmsworth, Doncaster, South Yorkshire, DN4 9QL.

Great Northern Books
PO Box 213, Ilkley, LS29 9WS
www.greatnorthernbooks.co.uk

Photography © Bill Reed

ISBN: 978-0-9572951-7-9

Design and layout: David Burrill

CIP Data
A catalogue for this book is available from the British Library

Printed and bound in India by Replika Press Pvt. Ltd.

THIS BOOK IS DEDICATED TO
MARY REED (1928 - 2002)

INTRODUCTION

All of the pictures in this book were taken during the late 1950s and early 1960s by Bill Reed on several of his trips north of the border. As steam was declining in Britain, he made the dash, along with many others, to Scotland to see, marvel and photograph locomotives still in operation there on the area's many branch lines and at a number of key works and sheds. Bill also took the pictures when it was a privilege, not to mention a rarity, to have a decent camera.

In excess of 500 colour slides were scanned and a final batch of over 200 was chosen. Suffice to say it was a very difficult decision knowing what to leave out. A number of images have required slight contrast and colour adjustments as well as the removal of unwanted dust and scratch marks. But, for the most part, many remain as fresh as the day they were actually taken. For ease of reference and with Bill's permission an A - Z format for the book was decided upon. Thus quite a wide area is covered from Glasgow to Garelochhead, Oban to Inverness, and Inverurie to Edinburgh.

None of the pictures were taken on organised visits to works or sheds even though the presence of non railway staff in some of the images may suggest otherwise. Travelling from his home in Nottingham, Bill sometimes journeyed north on the back of a friend's motorbike or used his free rail passes to underpin the finance for the trips. Unfortunately on one of his return visits, he was involved in a road accident though this did nothing to curb his enthusiasm for a return visit the following year.

The pictures show he had free access to many locations and was unhindered by authority or red tape. We see evidence of this time and time again particularly at Edinburgh Haymarket, Glasgow St Rollox and Glasgow Polmadie. Judging from the number of rail staff going about their business in certain locations or just taking a break (as at Kipps) it would appear that they too did not mind being captured on film.
In photographing locomotives Bill always behaved responsibly and his closeness to them hurtling past is sometimes breathtaking. This is witnessed in the line-side pictures at Beattock Sidings, and Crianlarch Lower and Upper stations. We also learn from many of the pictures, showing water cranes and gigantic coalers, what a labour intensive business it was keeping a steam locomotive active on the rails. Of course many of these features were swept away soon after the demise of steam yet remind us that they were once part of everyday railway life. Gazing at the walkways within the sheds we cannot help but be reminded of the grease and grime that was met on each visit but for most enthusiasts it was it was just sheer fun to be there amongst the locomotives.

I have noted in the text the history of many of the loco sheds and, where appropriate, their status today. I also present extensive histories of the locomotives where they were built, where allocated, work schedules and if known their final destinies. But what is remarkable about this book is the vast number of locomotive classes included. The task of documenting them was enormous as the long bibliography at the back testifies.

The new 'green' diesels shown here look remarkably modern and more efficient than their steam counterparts, and that is why they have been included – as a stark contrast to their predecessors. But many of them have in turn given way to electrics in the intervening years.

Bill Reed was born in Nottingham in 1933. His interest in railways goes back to his early childhood when his mother used to take him to visit her sister's in Hucknall, travelling from Bulwell on the Sentinel Steam Railcars no. 5192 *Rising Sun* and no. 51908 *Expedition*. His grandfather was a retired driver, formerly on the MS&LR at Northwich. He came to Annesley, near Nottingham, to work on the GCR when it opened. Bill's father was also interested in transport, having been apprenticed at Broughs, the Bulwell motorcycle builders, and after the Second World War he worked at Wrigley's Wagon Repair Works in Nottingham. He also had an allotment, conveniently situated at the side of the Great Central line, overlooking Bulwell Common Sidings. To Bill it was a train-spotter's paradise, and he bought his first stock book, Ian Allan's *ABC of British Locomotives*, in 1943. On leaving school, the only job Bill could find with the railways was as a messenger lad at Nottingham Victoria Station enquiry office, earning 39s a week. Bill spent his lunch hours on platforms at Victoria Station where he first met Freddie Guildford, a well known local railway enthusiast. Freddie knew all the Colwick drivers and many others too. His enthusiasm was infectious. He encouraged Bill to take photographs, but the latter's only camera was a Kodak 127 with perforated bellows. Freddie also showed Bill how to develop films and make contact prints.

By January 1950 Bill was getting fed up with waiting for a transfer to Annesley Loco Depot, so he went to the Midland Region at Middle Furlong Road. There he was immediately able to obtain a job as an engine cleaner, the first step in the long slow haul to be a driver. The progress was interrupted by National Service, when Bill was drafted to the Royal Corps of Signals and sent to Singapore.

Bill enjoyed guard duty at the Singapore military hospital since it was at the side of a main line with passenger trains to Kuala Lumpur. He took photographs at the shed in Singapore, but he was reminded of home when passing through the Suez Canal, seeing a Class 04 2-8-0 and an 8F 2-8-0 working trains.

On being demobbed Bill bought an Agfa Super Isolette, which in 1955 was considered a very good camera. He has used it to take most of his collection and still sometimes uses it today. Bill returned to work at British Rail as a fireman, and besides firing on normal runs to such places as Crewe and Wellingborough, he went on

excursions to Cleethorpes, Blackpool, Dudley Zoo and South Lynn. Generally, the locomotives he worked on were 4Fs, 8Fs and Class 5s. In 1966 he was passed for driving, but had to wait 13 years before being made a regular driver. By that time, steam had given way to diesel.

In later years, most of his black and white photography was done with a Mamiya 330, but he also had 35mm Practicas, a Canon for colour, and a Bolex 8mm cine.

Looking back now at the 1950s and 1960s, Bill says he would have taken many more pictures of steam locomotives in and around Scotland. But that is no matter, he has taken enough to give us more than a hint of what it was like in those last days of Scottish steam.

This book is dedicated to the memory of Bill's wife Mary (1928 - 2002), who formed a unique 'railway' partnership with him. Whenever they were out on a photographic mission, and this could be anywhere in the world, they shared camera duties. But she, for the most part, filmed locomotives, whilst Bill took colour or b/w pictures of them.

ABERDEEN FERRYHILL SHED NO. 60530

Peppercorn A2 Pacific no. 60530 *Sayajirao* is running on the line that ran past the coal stage to Aberdeen Ferryhill shed's 70ft. turntable. This feature was added in the south east corner of the site during 1908 and replaced a 50ft. example. Also, seen to the right of the locomotive is the shed's old water tank, which was provided when the first shed was built in April 1850. A new tank was added at the time of the installation of the turntable. In *LMS Engine Sheds Volume Five* (1987) it is noted that in 1916 the shed was consuming 52 million gallons of water annually, which was provided by Aberdeen Corporation. *Sayajirao* was a visitor to the shed, possibly from one of the Edinburgh depots (Haymarket or St. Margaret's) as the later BR emblem the wrong way round indicates the picture dates from the late-1950s to early-1960s. The locomotive could have headed a passenger service but it was more likely to have been a goods working. No. 60530 spent 16 of its 18 years in service working in Scotland.

ABERDEEN FERRYHILL 60006

Taking on water at the north end of Ferryhill shed is a member of Gresley's A4 Class. The shed was built by the North British Railway in 1908 and the brick building was a ten track straight shed adjoined by a two track repair shop. Caledonian Railway locomotives also used the shed and paid the NBR rent, with this arrangement being the cause of much dispute over the years. The locomotive, no. 60006 *Sir Ralph Wedgwood*, was built at Doncaster Works for the London & North Eastern Railway in January 1938 but was originally numbered 4466 and named *Herring Gull*. At this time the locomotive was fitted with a streamlined non-corridor tender, no. 5670, which gave the locomotive a total length of 71ft. 3⅛in. and wheelbase of 60ft. 10⅝in. The capacity of the tender was 5,000 gallons of water and nine tons of coal. The locomotive changed its name in January 1944 after the original bearer of the name, no. 4469, was damaged beyond repair after a German bomb detonated close by when it was in York north's no. 4 shed on 29 April 1942. No. 60006 reported for duty at Aberdeen during May 1964 and spent 16 months in service from the shed.

ABERDEEN FERRYHILL 69224

No. 69224, originally carrying LNER no. 9227, was the final engine of the N15 class to be built and it was part of an order for twenty that was placed by the LNER at Cowlairs Works after Grouping. This order was to prove the final task for Cowlairs in regard to construction, as upon completion of no. 9227 the works switched from construction to the maintenance of LNER-owned locomotives. Despite being built for the LNER, the 20 locomotives followed the NBR A Class 0-6-2T design. No. 69224 was built with steam brakes so was classified N15/1. The locomotive is pictured near the coal stage at Aberdeen Ferryhill shed, but it was only a 'foreigner' at this time as it was allocated to Keith shed (March 1958 to March 1959). It would become a resident at Ferryhill from the latter date to June 1961, moving to St. Margaret's shed to see out its career. This ended in October 1962 and the engine was amongst the final class withdrawals.

ABERDEEN FERRYHILL 69127

Ferryhill shed was located just to the south of Ferryhill Junction. This was where the Great North of Scotland Railway line from Ballater, opened in the mid-1860s, met the Aberdeen Railway line (later CR) to Guthrie, which had been completed in the early-1850s. To the north of the junction the first permanent terminus was opened in August 1854 and named Aberdeen Guild Street station. This was replaced by a joint station opened by the GNSR and CR on 4 November 1867. Aberdeen Joint station was rebuilt in 1915 and has seen alterations in the early part of this century. Pictured at Ferryhill shed's coal stage is a former NBR A Class 0-6-2T, no. 69127. The locomotive was constructed by the North British Locomotive Company's Hyde Park Works in June 1910 as part of an order for six that were equipped with Westinghouse brake equipment only. Six of the class had been constructed previously and a further 53 were produced before Grouping; 30 after. The LNER split the A Class into two classifications; N14 and N15 (itself divided into two sub-classifications) depending on their brake equipment. No. 69127 fell into the N15/2 classification, but subsequently had its Westinghouse apparatus removed and replaced with steam brakes with vacuum ejector in October 1953. The locomotive was withdrawn from Ferryhill shed in June 1959.

ABERDEEN KITTYBREWSTER 40573

Pictured in storage after it was withdrawn in May 1959, is a Fowler 2P 4-4-0, which was constructed at Derby Works in May 1928. The locomotive had a long-term allocation to Hurlford and could be at Kittybrewster waiting for transferral to Inverurie Works to be dismantled. The J37 behind, no. 64560, was built by the NBLC during July 1918 and from Nationalisation was present at Dunfermline. The engine could be waiting for repair by Inverurie as the locomotive did not leave service until March 1961.

ABERDEEN KITTYBREWSTER 55185

The first shed at Kittybrewster was opened on 12 September 1854 by the Great North of Scotland Railway. The building was a four track straight shed sited on the west side of Kittybrewster station. At the turn of the century the GNSR replaced the straight shed with a half-roundhouse that incorporated stalls for stabling 18 locomotives. BR switched the use of the depot to diesel engines in June 1961, however, it was later demolished and the site is now used by Aberdeen Council. This CR 439 Class engine was visiting Aberdeen from Keith, its home between October 1952 and July 1961 - its date of withdrawal.

ABERDEEN KITTYBREWSTER SHED 44312

The high point of construction for the LMS Fowler 4F 0-6-0 Class was between 1924 and 1928 when 531 examples were erected. A number of works were involved in the production of 4Fs and these were; Derby, NBLC, Kerr, Stuart & Co., Crewe, St Rollox, Andrew Barclay Sons & Co. and Horwich. The design was based on the Midland Railway's 3835 Class, also designed by Fowler and the 4Fs deviated relatively little from their predecessors. However, the 4Fs did have increased route availability, left hand drive (from 1925) and Ross pop safety valves. Stanier later approved an order for forty-four 4Fs and these were constructed at Crewe and Derby between 1937 and 1941 with only very slight detail differences. No. 44312 was the first of a batch of 20 to be built by St Rollox Works between 1927 and 1928 and the engine entered traffic in November 1927. From Nationalisation until its withdrawal the locomotive was allocated to Hurlford shed. Based on its condition and distance from its home shed it could be assumed that the engine was a recent visitor to Inverurie Works.

ABERDEEN KITTYBREWSTER 80029

BR Standard Class 4 2-6-4T locomotive no. 80029 was constructed at Brighton Works in January 1952 and was destined for the Scottish Region along with ten others erected at the works as part of order no. BR3621. No. 80029 was one of four from this batch allocated to Kittybrewster when new and they replaced a number of former Great North of Scotland Railway 4-4-0s. The class members at the shed could be employed on passenger and goods services to Fraserburgh and Ballater, with main line services to Inverness a task sometime allotted to them. Eighteen Standard Class 4 2-6-4Ts spent time at Kittybrewster shed; no. 80020 was the first to arrive in October 1951, while the last was no. 80013 in June 1957, which came from Polmadie. Two of the class left in November 1955, the first to do so, and dispersal continued until June 1961 when seven were left to be moved on when the shed closed to steam. Two found their way to Ferryhill but this was only a brief arrangement. The class were originally fitted with LNER-style return cranks with square crank pins and these were joined together by means of two vertical bolts. However, these were later substituted for the LMS-style on later new examples of the class and the return cranks were secured to the crank pins by four studs and bolts. No. 80029 is fitted with the LNER arrangement as well as fluted coupling rods; some later engines were fitted with rectangular ones. The locomotive left Kittybrewster in June 1961 and relocated to Ardrossan where it was resident for a year. The engine then worked from Hurlford until withdrawn in December 1965 and it was subsequently sold to Shipbreaking Industries, Faslane, to be scrapped.

ABERFELDY STATION 55200

Aberfeldy station was opened by the Inverness & Perth Junction Railway on 3 July 1865. It was the terminus of the branch line from Ballinluig on the Perth - Inverness route. Running up a valley to the town of Aberfeldy, the branch line was closed to freight in March 1965 and then to passengers in May of that year. From Ballinluig Junction to Aberfeldy the line was signalled by traditional semaphore from signalboxes until closure. The station building and locomotive shed have been demolished and the vacated station area is currently a parking space. Also, the trackbed has been infilled to the level of the platform. Caledonian Railway 439 Class 0-4-4T, no. 55200, was designed by John Farquharson McIntosh (1846-1918) and built at St Rollox, Glasgow in 1909. Ninety-two engines of the class were erected between 1900 and 1925, a few under LMS auspices. Seventy-four Class 439s passed into British Railways ownership in 1948 and they were numbered 55159-55236 (with gaps). No. 55200's last shed was 63A Perth, before withdrawal to Inverurie Works in November 1961.

BALLACHULISH STATION 55204

Situated on the south shore of Loch Leven at Glencoe in the Highlands, the station was opened as Ballachulish on 20 August 1903 by the Callander & Oban Railway. With two platforms, a goods shed (behind the loco), and a locomotive shed, the station was the terminus of the former branch from Connel Ferry (on the line to Oban). The station was renamed in 1905 as Ballachulish & Glencoe, three years later as Ballachulish (Glencoe) for Kinlochleven and apart from a short closure in 1953, this latter name remained until final closure in March 1966. The locomotive shed was timber built with two roads and the facilities included a coaling stage, water tank and 60ft. turntable. It was officially closed in 1962. The track bed has been filled in to platform level and the station was used for a time as a garage, but is presently a doctor's surgery. The former slate quarries – behind the main station building - were served by a line extending from the goods yard (off to the left) and a number of narrow gauge lines. CR 439 Class 0-4-4T, no. 55204, was designed by McIntosh and built at St Rollox, Glasgow in 1910. No. 55204's last shed was 63A Perth, before withdrawal in December 1962. The engine moved to Motherwell Machinery & Scrap, Wishaw, for dismantling in December 1964.

BANFF STATION 55221

No doubt it was a precarious proposition attaining this photograph (on the left) of CR 439 Class locomotive no. 55221. Banff is located in Aberdeenshire and the first railway to operate from the town was the Banff, Portsoy & Strathisla Railway, which reached Grange and the Inverness - Aberdeen Line in 1859. The BPSR line was just over 16 miles long and stops in between the two places included; Ladysbridge, Tillynaught, Cornhill, Glenbarry and Knock. Due to financial problems the line was taken over by the GNSR in 1867. The station at Banff was originally a temporary structure, opened in July 1859, but this had been superseded by a permanent building opened on 1 May 1860. No. 55221 was manufactured at St Rollox Works in August 1914. The locomotive was working from Keith shed at the time of this picture and had been allocated there in August 1953. This lasted until June 1961 when it moved to Corkerhill shed, Glasgow and the engine was then withdrawn from there in October 1961. The line did not last much further into the 1960s as the section between Banff and Tillynaught closed on 6 July 1964 and the line was closed completely in 1968.

BATHGATE SHED 69159

This NBR A Class locomotive was built by the NBLC's Hyde Park Works in August 1912; seventeen of the class were built there during the month. The class were designed by William P. Reid (1854-1932), who was Locomotive Superintendent of the NBR between 1903 and 1919. Reid started his career as an apprentice at Cowlairs Works and rose through the ranks to succeed Matthew Holmes. The NBR A Class was just one of several designs he introduced in addition to modernising a number of older designs. When built, this locomotive was assigned NBR no. 922 and later received LNER no. 9922, which was carried from November 1924. The engine was classified N15/1 by the latter company as it had steam brakes only and remained unmodified in this respect for the rest of its career. BR no. 69159 was applied from July 1948 and at this time the locomotive was allocated to Bathgate shed and had possibly been there since 1935. The shed employed the members of the class based there on mainly shunting duties, although at one time they had been responsible for hauling coal trains. No. 69159 was withdrawn from its duties at the shed in October 1961 but was not scrapped at Arnott Young's scrapyard at Carmyle until June 1963; it spent some of the intervening time stored at the shed.

BATHGATE SHED 68102 AND 68118

Bathgate is located in West Lothian; five miles west of Livingston and approximately 20 miles to the west of Edinburgh. A number of railway companies operated in the area between the mid-1820s and mid-1840s, however, they focussed on freight and mineral traffic from the mines in the area. The first company to have an interest in passenger traffic as well as in an industrial capacity was the Edinburgh and Bathgate Railway, who opened their line in November 1849. It ran from Ratho to the east of the town and Bathgate Junction with the Edinburgh and Glasgow Railway line to Bathgate station. This was the location for the first shed, which was opened at the same time and contained two roads. The EBR became a part of the NBR in 1865 and at this time a new station was constructed slightly to the west of the original and known as Bathgate Upper. The shed was replaced in 1902 with a six road building that lasted until 1954 when replaced owing to subsidence. Two 0-4-0ST locomotives of the NBR Class G, LNER Y9 Class, are seen at the shed after they had been withdrawn from St. Margaret's shed. Nos. 68102 and 68118 were both built at Cowlairs Works in January 1891 and December 1897 respectively for light shunting duties. No. 68118 is still attached to its four wheel coal carrier, which increased the capacity from the insignificant 18 cwt available on the locomotive. No. 68118 left service in October 1958, whilst no. 68102 followed two months later. Bathgate Upper station closed on 9 January 1956 with the shed closing in August 1966. The station reopened in the mid-1980s as part of a regeneration of the area.

BEATTOCK SIDINGS 72000

Heading a 'down' through freight is BR Standard Class 6 'Clan' Pacific no. 72000 *Clan Buchanan*. The locomotive has passed Beattock North signal box and from here the locomotive starts its ten mile journey to Beattock Summit - the highest point on the west coast main line. The gradients of the climb vary between 1 in 69 and 1 in 88 to the summit, which is 1016ft. above sea level and 52 miles from Glasgow. Having passed through the west side loop line at Beattock station *Clan Buchanan* is likely to have picked up a banking engine to aid its assent to the summit. After it was constructed at Crewe Works in December 1951, the locomotive was allocated to Polmadie shed and would have worked to Carlisle and Preston though workings as far south as Liverpool and Manchester were possible. Internal Scottish workings included turns to Stranraer, Edinburgh, Perth and Dundee. No. 72000 was amongst a number of 'Clans' that were allocated to Edinburgh Haymarket in November 1957 and from there they could find work over the Waverley route and to Heaton. *Clan Buchanan* returned to Polmadie in March 1960 and was relieved of its duties in December 1962 and scrapped at Darlington Works in February 1964.

BEATTOCK STATION 55234

CR Class 439 locomotive no. 55234 had made quite a journey from Aberdeen Ferryhill shed for its new allocation at Beattock just after Nationalisation. It remained at the shed until withdrawn in December 1962. The main work for engines stationed at Beattock shed was banking freight and passenger trains up to Beattock Summit on the west coast main line. Local passenger and freight, especially livestock movement, were also undertaken; no. 55234 is destined for Moffat with this freight service. Originally 2-4-0s and 0-4-2 locomotives were to be found banking before 0-4-4Ts became the norm and several could be found at Beattock from the 1920s up to the mid-1950s.

BEATTOCK SHED 57618

The Caledonian Railway line between Glasgow and Carlisle received Royal Assent on 31 July 1845. Twenty thousand men were involved in the construction of the 90 (approx.) mile-long route as well as the line between Carstairs and Edinburgh. Inspection of the line from Carlisle to Beattock was carried out by Board of Trade Inspecting Officer Captain Simmonds on 4 September 1847 and the section was opened on 10 September, with coaches conveying passengers the remaining distance to Glasgow. The line became fully operational on 15 February 1848. The shed had been constructed at the same time as the station and they shared the same date of opening with the line. The shed was constructed from stone with a gable roof and had a 42ft. turntable and coal stage; all located at the north end of the station and on the west side of the Caledonian line. The locomotive pictured is a CR 812 Class 0-6-0, built by St Rollox Works in September 1899. Seventy-nine were constructed at four works; Dübs & Co., Neilson, Reid & Co., Sharp, Stewart & Co. and St Rollox. A further 17 were built to a similar design and known as the CR 652 Class. No. 57618 was allocated to Carstairs when the photograph was taken and was withdrawn while at the shed during March 1962. Beattock shed was closed by BR on 1 May 1967 and the station closed on 3 January 1972. The station's closure was due to the electrification of the northern section of the west coast main line, which was approved in March 1970 and completed in May 1974. There are currently efforts to have the station reopened.

BLAIR ATHOLL STATION 54486

The station was initially referred to as Blair Athole when opened by the Inverness & Perth Junction Railway on 9 September 1863. The railway's line ran between the Inverness & Aberdeen Junction Railway at Forres and the Perth and Dunkeld Railway at Dunkeld and it was completed in three sections. The station was on the third section of the route to be opened between Aviemore and Pitlochry. The I&PJR became a part of the Highland Railway from 1 February 1865 and the latter company changed the station's name from September 1893 to its present title. A CR Class 72 4-4-0 locomotive has been pictured at the station sometime in the late-1950s to early-1960s. Manufacture of the engine was carried out by St Rollox Works in September 1920 to the design of William Pickersgill, who was the final Locomotive Superintendent of the CR and had held the position since 1914. The engine had 6ft. 6in. diameter driving wheels and two inside cylinders with Stephenson motion. Perth was no. 54486's last shed and it was taken out of service in February 1962 after being there under four years.

BURNMOUTH STATION 64925

Burnmouth station was opened between 1846 and 1848 by the North British Railway on the Edinburgh to Berwick-upon-Tweed line, which itself was opened for services from 23 July 1846. The station was the last before the line crossed the border with England and was 52 miles from Edinburgh, 72 from Newcastle and 340 miles from London. The three mile long Eyemouth branch line that is acknowledged on the sign was authorised in 1884, but was not completed until 13 April 1891 and was operated by the Eyemouth Railway. It was taken over by the NBR in 1900. No. 64925 is seen with the service to Eyemouth in this photograph. Burnmouth and Eyemouth stations were closed on 5 February 1962.

BURNMOUTH STATION 64925

LNER Gresley J39 Class 0-6-0 locomotive no. 64925 has been pictured at Burnmouth station. The engine was erected by Beyer, Peacock & Co. in April 1937 and was amongst nine of the class completed there during the year and 28 overall. The J39's were sub-classified according to the type of tender they carried and no. 64925 was in class part one as these engines had group standard 3,500 gallon tenders with a 5½ ton coal capacity. The tenders built by Beyer, Peacock & Co. were different to other group standard 3,500 gallon tenders as they were fabricated by welding. Another variation in the tenders of class part one was that the coping plate protruded at the top of the side sheet. No. 64925 was also fitted with vacuum brakes and the reservoir for the system can be seen at the rear of the tender. The locomotive was amongst the final J39 Class withdrawals in December 1962 and all of the class were scrapped.

CARSTAIRS SHED 76002

Built at Horwich Works in December 1952, the locomotive was the third of the class to appear and entered traffic in December 1952 to Motherwell shed - 66B. The first five were sent to work at the shed but two of the locomotives, no. 76000 and 76002, did not get off to a good start as both were in accidents during December. No. 76002 was in a collision between Glasgow and Hamilton damaging its motion and was out of action at Doncaster Works until March 1953. When the engine returned to Motherwell it would have been employed on local passenger services around Glasgow and to the Clyde coast as well as freight destined for places as far afield as Perth, Forfar and Aberdeen. The Standard Class 4 2-6-0s were fitted with BR7 boilers, which were tapered, fitted with dome mounted regulators and worked at 225psi. The boiler originally fitted to no. 76002 was built at Darlington, with Doncaster, Swindon and Crewe also manufacturing them. A BR2 tender was also fitted upon completion of construction and it had a capacity of 3,500 gallons of water and six tons of coal. The tender appears to be fitted with a draught excluder, which were added after the locomotives had been in service. No. 76002 spent its entire career at Motherwell as did its classmates - no. 76000 and 76003.

CARSTAIRS SHED 42173

Carstairs resident no. 42173 poses outside the shed. The locomotive emerged from Derby Works in October 1948 to the design of Charles Fairburn. He had introduced the first example of this 2-6-4T design in March 1945 shortly before his death in October and construction of the class continued into 1951 when a total of 277 had been produced. The first shed at Carstairs was built on the north side of the station in 1848, but it only lasted until 1853 when replaced by a four track timber shed. The Caledonian Railway installed both structures and added a coal stage and 50ft. turntable in 1860 and 1896 respectively. Complete renovation of the shed was completed by the LMS in 1935 at an estimated cost of £24,048. The shed was remade using bricks, retaining the same number of tracks, and a 75 ton mechanical coaler as well as an ash disposal capability were included in the new layout. No. 42173 was allocated to Carstairs between 1950 and December 1962 - the time of its withdrawal.

CONNEL FERRY STATION 55208

Seen at Connel Ferry station's former 'up' platform, with the Ballachulish branch passenger service, is CR McIntosh 439 or Standard Passenger Class 0-4-4T locomotive no. 55208. The station was located on the Callander & Oban Railway line between the two towns and later was also the changing place for the service to Ballachulish, which was reached by a branch line. Connel Ferry station was opened on 1 July 1880 and was at first small in size, but it was later enlarged in 1903 with the installation of an island platform, which was due to the addition of services for Ballachulish. In the distance, behind the last carriage, is the west signal box, which was one of two. They were erected during the enlargement of the station and the west signal box had 56 levers, while the east had 42. They were in use until closed on 8 January 1967.

CONNEL FERRY 55208

This locomotive is also pictured on the 'down' main line with the Ballachulish branch passenger service, while some livestock wagons are seen on the goods loop line. No. 55208 was built at St Rollox Works in March 1911, entering the 439 Class as CR no. 153. Subsequently the locomotive was numbered 15208 by the LMS before acquiring its BR number after Nationalisation. At this time the locomotive was allocated to Perth shed and it remained there until April 1955, transferring to Oban to see out the remainder of its career, which ended in October 1961. It was scrapped at Inverurie Works during February 1962.

CONNEL FERRY STATION 55204

A view of no. 55204 from the station footbridge on the island platform side looking south onto the 'down' main line and the goods loop line. The station goods yard was on the north side of the station and also featured a turntable. More goods sidings were installed on the south side during the Second World War however, these had been removed by 1950. After the closure of the Ballachulish branch the island platform was taken out of use and the original platform regained its prominence. The island platform was removed in the mid-1980s and the station buildings have also been removed and replaced with a shelter. The goods yard has become an oil distribution centre.

CONNEL FERRY STATION 45482

LMS Stanier Class Five or 'Black Five' 4-6-0 no. 45482 was built at Derby Works in September 1943 and was one of 54 Class Fives to be produced at the works between April 1943 and December 1944. These engines featured a number of modifications that included; additional cross stays at the horns, fluted coupling rods, shorter connecting rods and longer slidebars. The fitting of cross stays were an just one attempt to cure the problem of twisting and cracking of the frames of the engines, which was a persistent puzzle for the engineers at the LMS. The cross stays perpetuated the problem and it was not until rigorous tests were carried out that a satisfactory improvement was identified. From no. 4825 the frame was redesigned to use thicker frame plates and hornblocks; the lack of the latter and use of axlebox guides in their place being a cause of the cracking problem. The use of no. 45482 was discontinued from June 1964.

CONNEL FERRY 55263

The Callander and Oban Railway was formed in 1864, but construction of the line did not begin until 1866 and not completed until 1880. A number of junctions with other companies were also present on the line and included; Lochearnhead, St. Fillans and Comrie Railway, Killin Railway and the West Highland Railway. No. 55263 was a continuation of the McIntosh 439 Class design, but was built by the LMS in May 1925 and was one of ten completed. No. 55263 was a long-time resident at Oban shed, noted there from at least Nationalisation until withdrawn in November 1961. The C&OR line between Callander and Crianlarich closed on 27 September 1965 after a landslide. The line between Oban and Crianlarich Junction with the former West Highland Railway still continues to operate.

CRAIGELLACHIE STATION SC79970

The service to Elgin, from Aviemore, has stopped at Craigellachie station. From the station this BR Railbus, SC79970, would have taken the former Morayshire Railway line at Craigellachie Junction, which would have led it to Elgin. SC79970 was built by Park Royal Vehicles, who mainly produced buses for London Transport. The company only built five Railbuses to the design and initially they were going to work London Midland Region lines, however, Scotland was soon chosen to be their place of operation. SC79970 entered traffic in February 1959 and was working from Leith before it found itself further north. It was fitted with a AEC six cylinder horizontal engine that developed 150bhp. It was 42ft. long, 9ft. 3in. wide, weighed 15 tons and could seat 50 people. SC79970 was withdrawn in March 1967 and scrapped by September. The station was the second to hold the name Craigellachie. It was opened by the Strathspey Railway on 1 July 1863, however, was at first known as Strathspey Junction. Eleven months later it became Craigellachie Junction but it dropped the latter part in 1872. In mid-1866 the line became part of the GNSR. The station closed on 6 May 1968.

CRAIGELLACHIE STATION GNSR 49 AND HR 103

On 16 June 1962 this image was captured at Craigellachie featuring Great North of Scotland Railway Class F 4-4-0 locomotive no. 49 *Gordon Highlander* and Highland Railway 'Jones Goods' Class 4-6-0 no. 103. The former engine was built by the NBLC in October 1920 and along with GNSR Class V, no. 49 became part of LNER Class D40, which totalled 21. As BR no. 62277 the locomotive was withdrawn in June 1958 and preserved by the company to work railtours. No. 103 was amongst 15 built by Sharp, Stewart & Co. between September and November 1894. The locomotive was absorbed by the LMS at Grouping, becoming no. 17916, but it was withdrawn by the company in 1934; BR restored the locomotive in 1959. Both locomotives are operating as part of the Stephenson Locomotive Society and Railway Correspondence &Travel Society's Joint Scottish Tour. It had begun on the 14th and lasted to the 23rd, starting at Perth and taking in places, amongst others, such as; Inverness, Thurso, Wick, Forres, Aviemore, Keith, Aberdeen, Bridge of Dun, Forfar, Blairgowrie, Gleneagles, Stirling, Thornton Junction, Glasgow, Dumfries and it finished at Carlisle. A number of other locomotives were also involved with the tour and they included; LMS Fairburn 2-6-4T, LMS Hughes 'Crab', LMS 'Black Five', CR McIntosh 439 Class, CR Drummond 'Jumbo', CR McIntosh 812 Class, NBR Reid Class B, NBR Holmes Class C, LNER Gresley J38 Class, BR Standard Class 2 2-6-0 and BR Standard Class 4 2-6-4T. No. 49 and no. 103 are in front of two preserved CR coaches, nos. 1375 and 464, a Third Class Compartment and First/Third/Brake Corridor Composite. The locomotives were retired in 1966 and took up residence at the Glasgow Museum of Transport, while the coaches later found their way to the Scottish Railway Preservation Society; no. 49 joined them on loan in 2011.

CRIANLARICH LOWER STATION 44923

Crianlarich station was opened by the Callander and Oban Railway on 1 August 1873 with two platforms and sidings. The north platform was removed during November 1921 when the station was under the direction of the CR. The 'Lower' potion of the station's title was added by BR, but the company subsequently closed the station on 28 September 1965. The station building has been latterly replaced with a village hall. The Stanier 'Black Five' featured in the photograph was a product of Crewe Works and entered traffic in January 1946. No. 44923 was one of ten, later extended to a further 14 locomotives, that were experimentally fitted with manganese steel liners for the axleboxes and horns. This was done because the white metal used previously was prone to wear and knocking. The result was a dramatic improvement and new locomotives were consequently fitted with this new arrangement and some older members of the class were also modified. No. 44923's career came to an end in June 1964.

CRIANLARICH UPPER STATION 44957

A 21 year gap existed between the opening of the first and second stations that served Crianlarich. This station was on the West Highland Railway and it was open for services on 7 August 1894. The WHR line was started on 23 October 1889 and completed at the time of the station's opening, linking Fort William with Craigendoran Junction and the lines to Glasgow. The station site included; an island platform, refreshment room, locomotive shed, goods sidings and a crossing loop on the south side of the platform. BR added the 'Upper' portion of the station's title during 1951, but unlike Crianlarich Lower station, Crianlarich Upper remains open and reverted back to just Crianlarich in the second half of the 1960s.

This Stanier Class Five, seen with the 09.31 service from Fort William to Glasgow Queen Street, was built at Horwich Works in May 1946. At this time the engine was attached to tender no. 10582, of the Mark One part welded variety with a capacity of nine tons of coal and 4,000 gallons of water. In August of the year following construction, no. 44957 possessed a Mark Two tender, which was manufactured using welding. The engine continued to be paired to this type until it left service. A number of Class Fives were stationed at Eastfield shed during the 1950s and 1960s to work in the West Highland area and no. 44957 was present there from December 1954 until moving on to Corkerhill in January 1963. The engine moved again in March to Dumfries and was withdrawn from there in May 1964. When the engine was made it was fitted with boiler no. 12346, which had a sloping firebox throatplate and 28 element superheater. During the war years the elements were the Superheater Company's double return type and had replaced bifurcated elements that had been used previously. From 1946 this latter type was reintroduced by the LMS and they were 1¼in. diameter, however, BR discontinued the use of bifurcated elements on locomotives constructed from 1949. No. 44957 was also involved in the trial fitting of manganese steel axlebox liners.

DINGWALL SHED GWR 1649

Dingwall shed was only a small facility that was located to the south of the station and on the west side of the line to Conon station (now closed). Erected by the Highland Railway in 1870, the structure was made from wood and a gable roof covered two roads that were accessible from the north end. At this end a turntable was provided, however, this was removed by the LMS sometime in the 1930s. In the shed yard is GWR no. 1649 manufactured at Swindon Works in May 1951. The locomotive belonged to the 1600 Class design for a 0-6-0PT, which was prepared by the final GWR Chief Mechanical Engineer Frederick Hawksworth. However, none of the engines entered service for the GWR as construction began in 1949 and continued to 1955 when 70 were in existence. The locomotive has a pannier tank as it uses a Belpaire firebox, which is not readily compatible with a saddle tank design. No. 1649 had 4ft. 1½in. diameter driving wheels, a water capacity of 875 gallons, two inside cylinders with Stephenson motion with slide valves; was 30ft. 2½in. in length and weighed 41 tons 12 cwt. The engine started its career at St Philip's Marsh shed, Bristol, before making the long trip to Helmsdale, its new residence, in July 1958 and joining its classmate no. 1646. No. 1649 was removed from its duties in December 1962 after a disappointingly short service life of 11½ years. The shed closed in December 1961 and no trace remains.

DINGWALL STATION 44978

Heading the Inverness to Wick portion of the 1962 Joint RCTS/SLS Scottish Rail Tour is 'Black Five' no. 44978. The locomotive was involved on the first three days of the tour taking it on the first day from Inverness to Muir of Ord, Dingwall, Achnasheen and Kyle of Lochalsh before starting a return. The following day the tour started again from Inverness to Muir of Ord and Dingwall then on to Brora and Georgemas Junction where HR 103 took the reins. Dingwall station was opened by the Inverness & Ross-shire Railway on 11 June 1862 on the company's new line between Inverness and the town, which was extended to Invergordon the following year. The company was short lived as soon after the station opened it amalgamated with the Inverness & Aberdeen Junction Railway. The station was later operated by the Highland Railway and then the LMS after grouping.

DUMBARTON CENTRAL STATION SC75628

The Caledonian & Dumbartonshire Junction Railway proposed to connect Balloch with Bowling in the mid-1840s and this was approved in 1846. The line opened on 15 July 1850 and with it was the first station in Dumbarton. However, the line was not connected to Glasgow by means of a railway until 31 May 1858 and at this time a new station was opened replacing the first. The present station was opened by the former company and the Lanarkshire & Dumbartonshire Junction Railway in 1896. The new station featured two island platforms supported on red brick arches with parapets, waiting room on the platform, along with other station buildings and booking office at street level. On 31 January 1984 the station received Category A Listed status. This British Railways Class 303 Electric Multiple Unit (EMU) is at the south side of the station looking west; the building on the right is on the Station Road/College Street corner and is now a pub called the Railway Tavern. The 303 Class (classified AM3 before TOPS) were built in response to the electrification of the Strathclyde area and 91 units of three cars were eventually built by Pressed Steel Co. Ltd, Paisley, between 1959 and 1961. The sets featured DTSO-MBSO-BDTSO vehicles; the one closest in the frame being the BDTSO type. Numbered SC75628, this carriage was 63ft. 11½in. long, weighed 38.4 tons and had 83 seats and was built as part of the first lot, no. 30581, of BDTSO vehicles between 1959/1960. Mechanical specifications for the set included four Metro-Vic 155kW traction motors developing 829hp, Gresley bogies, air brakes and a top speed of 75mph; the total length of the set was 199ft. 6in. and the total weight was 129.2 tons. Sets could be joined and it would appear that at least two are in this photograph. Fifty were refurbished in the 1980s, but seemingly this carriage was not among them and was probably scrapped by the end of the decade; the last was withdrawn in 2002 and one set has been preserved.

DUMFRIES SHED 70051

BR Standard Class 7 'Britannia' Pacific no. 70051 was completed at Crewe Works in August 1954, but was not named *Firth of Forth* until January 1955. The final five members of the class began their careers at Polmadie shed, Glasgow and all were named at St Rollox Works; the choices being firths and forths. From Polmadie shed the general duties of the 'Britannias' were passenger and goods trains taken north as far as Perth and south as far as Carlisle. When new, the locomotive was fitted with a Smith Stone speedometer, however, the connection from the rear crank pin to the cab is curiously missing in this photograph. *Firth of Forth* moved to Corkerhill in April 1962 but had left Scotland for Crewe North by October. Moves to Holyhead, Crewe North, Crewe South and Banbury followed during the next four years before *Firth of Forth* arrived at its last allocation - Carlisle Kingmoor. The locomotive left service in December 1967 and was scrapped at J. McWilliams scrapyard, Shettleston, during March 1968.

DUMFRIES SHED 57623

To the right of this Caledonian Railway McIntosh 812 Class 0-6-0 no. 57623 is Dumfries shed's engine hoist. This was located along the eastern perimeter of the site and had a capacity of 30 tons. No. 57623 was constructed at St Rollox Works in October 1899 as CR no. 288. The locomotive was a long-term resident at the shed, being noted there from Nationalisation to withdrawal in November 1961. Four other members of the CR 812 Class had long spells at the shed; nos. 57600, 57601, 57602, 57621.

DUMFRIES SHED 56327

The Glasgow, Dumfries & Carlisle Railway constructed two sheds for engines based in the town and it later merged with the Glasgow, Paisley, Kilmarnock & Ayr Railway in 1850 to form the Glasgow & South Western Railway. A new shed was not considered until the mid-1870s and subsequently John Armour & Son were chosen to carry out the building work for a price of just over £5,000. Opening during 1878, the shed contained six roads utilising stone for the walls. It remained little altered in the intervening years until it was closed in mid-1966. No. 56327, a CR McIntosh 782 Class 0-6-0T, was made at St Rollox Works during July 1910 and was given CR no. 436. The locomotive was at Carlisle Kingmoor for Nationalisation before making the relatively short trip to Dumfries for its final allocation in December 1953. The locomotive's last month in service was September 1959.

DUMFRIES SHED 40170

Illustrated here is a 2-6-2T locomotive designed by Stanier for the LMS and built by Derby Works in December 1937 as LMS no. 170. It entered Class 3P, of which 139 were erected for use on secondary passenger services and they utilised Stanier's taper boiler, which is seen in the picture. The diameter of the boiler was 4ft. 9in. before it tapered, reducing to 4ft. 2in. diameter. However, as with Stanier's other taper boilers they encountered problems with performance, but unlike the others, modifications did little to alleviate the problems. No. 40170 presents a clean appearance implying that it is ex-works, but the later BR emblem has been applied incorrectly. The locomotive had a prolonged residency at Dumfries and left service from the shed in January 1962. The site has subsequently been cleared and from 1993 has accommodated the Dumfries & Galloway Constabulary headquarters.

DUNDEE WEST SHED 73151

The mid-1820s witnessed the birth of the Dundee & Newtyle Railway, which would become the first railway to serve the city when it fully opened its 11½ mile-long line in April 1832. The next line to reach the city was the Dundee & Arbroath Railway, which was completed in 1840 and later became part of the Scottish North Eastern Railway. The Dundee & Perth Railway built the final line to reach the city, commencing services in May 1847, but prior to this had arranged to lease the D&NR in 1846. The former date also signalled the opening of the company's Seabraes shed, which was the forerunner of Dundee West shed. Seabraes shed was unusually rhomboidal in its proportions and contained three roads. The D&PR was active until 1863, when it became a part of the Scottish Central Railway, who in turn came under the ownership of the Caledonian Railway in the early 1880s. The CR were unimpressed with Seabraes shed and decided to replace it with a new facility slightly to the west of the original and on the north side of the approach line to Dundee West station. The new shed had eight through roads, coal stage, offices and turntable when opened in 1885; the latter being improved to a 70ft. example from Cowans Sheldon in the mid-1900s and sited close to the eastern entrance. Despite its size, the shed never enjoyed a large contingent of locomotives and after Nationalisation became a virtual extension of Tay Bridge shed (formerly of the LNER, located close by to the east) storing and providing cover for its locomotives. This BR Standard Class Five 4-6-0 is pictured on Dundee West's turntable in the latter part of the 1950s. No. 73151 was erected at Derby Works in April 1957 and was one of thirty to be fitted with British-Caprotti valve gear. The features of this included poppet valves, camboxes on top of the cylinders and worm gearbox on the return cranks. The locomotive had only one allocation, which was to St Rollox and it left service from there in August 1966 to later be scrapped by Motherwell Machinery and Scrap Co., Wishaw. Dundee West shed was refurbished to house and maintain DMU's, reopening in 1960, however, by 1985 the site had been cleared.

DUNFERMLINE 68101

This NBR Class G, LNER Y9 Class 0-4-0ST was erected at Cowlairs Works in 1889 and given NBR no. 346, later receiving no. 888 and then no. 1088 in a NBR renumbering scheme. The NBR rebuilt a number of the locomotives during the early part of the 20th century with new boilers with the position of the safety valves altered and the pattern of the coupling rod ends changed; this locomotive received this attention in December 1913. No. 68101 was employed at Dunfermline from the early 1930s and could be found shunting carriages at Dunfermline Upper station. For this duty the engine was fitted with a vacuum ejector during 1937, which was in addition to the steam brake fitted in 1928, replacing a hand brake. No. 68101 was one of the final surviving members of the class and was withdrawn in October 1962; the last one, no. 68095, went in December.

DUNFERMLINE 61770

The GNR Gresley H3 Class of 2-6-0s, LNER Class K2, were built with; 5ft. 8in. diameter driving wheels, two cylinders 20in. by 26in. with 10in. piston valves and Walschaerts valve gear. The boiler was 5ft. 6in. diameter and had a 24 element Robinson superheater. This engine was the first of 25 to be built by Kitson & Co. in June 1921, with two design modifications of this batch being the discontinuation of piston tail rods and the use of Ross pop safety valves. No. 61770 has also been modified to have a cab with a window, which was an alteration carried out on locomotives working in the Scottish Region; no. 61770 had it fitted in July 1952. The locomotive had allocations at Eastfield and Thornton Junction before moving to Dunfermline in September 1952. From the latter it could find employment on both passenger and goods services around the Edinburgh area. The engine was condemned in July 1959.

DUNFERMLINE 65928

Stood outside Dunfermline shed is LNER Gresley J38 Class 0-6-0 no. 65928. The locomotive was built by Darlington Works in April 1926, entering this relatively small class (35 members) towards the end of the series. All of the class carried a slightly altered boiler from the original for varying periods. No. 65928 had a later diagram 97 boiler fitted from March 1953 to June 1957, but is carrying the original design, diagram 97A, in this photograph. The engine was also initially fitted with steam reversing gear, however, this was replaced by screw reverse gear in May 1945 as the former was difficult to operate for the uninitiated. The locomotive received the dubious distinction of being one of the first two engines of the class to be withdrawn in December 1962.

EDINBURGH DALRY ROAD SHED 42807

Photographed on the south side of Edinburgh's Dalry Road engine shed is a former LMS locomotive belonging to George Hughes's 'Crab' Class of 2-6-0 locomotives. The engine emerged completed from Crewe Works in December 1928 as LMS no. 13107 and was one of ten, 13100-13109, to begin their career at Perth North shed between December 1928 and January 1929. After several years at Carlisle Kingmoor the locomotive arrived at Dalry Road in May 1942 and did not move again until March 1961 when it was transferred to Ayr. In December 1962 the locomotive was sent to be broken up.

EDINBURGH DALRY ROAD SHED 57654

This locomotive has been pictured in front of the shed's old mess room that utilised a water tank for its roof. The first shed was constructed on the site during 1848 and a two track shed was later opened by the CR in 1874. This latter was converted to be a wagon repair shop, which was demolished in 1930. A four track shed was erected in 1895 before it was rebuilt in 1911 by James Kinnear at a cost of approx. £5,190. This CR Pickersgill 0-6-0 was made at St Rollox Works in July 1919 and was one of only two of the class present at Dalry Road shed under BR until withdrawn in April 1962. In October 1965 the shed was closed and was demolished in 1966, with the former CR lines around Dalry Road now forming the route of the West Approach Road.

EDINBURGH HAYMARKET SHED 62743

The Gresley D49 Class of 4-4-0s were built for work on secondary passenger services in the north of England and Scotland and to replace a number of the constituent companies life-expired classes. Darlington Works was the only works to produce the D49s and this example, no. 62743 *The Cleveland*, entered traffic in August 1932; one of two class members completed during the month. *The Cleveland* is photographed at south side of the west end of Edinburgh Haymarket sometime in the mid-1950s and is on one of the two ash pit tracks at the shed. Cleaning the fire was an unenviable task carried out by labourers and it appears to be well underway here. The smokebox has probably already been cleaned with remnants of the contents visible below the door. From the ash pits *The Cleveland* would have been moved to one of the shed roads to be prepared for its next service. The locomotive had begun its allocation at Haymarket during January 1951 and was still housed at the shed when it was removed from service in May 1960.

EDINBURGH HAYMARKET SHED 60536

Approaching Haymarket shed from the west is Peppercorn A2 Class Pacific no. 60536 *Trimbush*, which was constructed at Doncaster Works in May 1948. When Edward Thompson retired as Chief Mechanical Engineer of the LNER, 15 A2 Class (later A2/3) locomotives were still to be built, however, they were redesigned by the new CME, A.H. Peppercorn. The locomotives featured a new boiler, repositioned cylinders, single chimney, self-cleaning smokebox and 'banjo' dome with perforated steam collector. *Trimbush* started its career at Leeds Copley Hill shed but quickly switched to Peterborough New England shed and was then sent to Haymarket in November 1949. This allocation lasted until November 1961 when it spent several months at St. Margaret's only to return in May 1962. It was sent back to St. Margaret's in October only to be withdrawn in December.

EDINBURGH HAYMARKET SHED 68457

No. 68457 appears to have experienced a rough shunt as the front footplating is slightly distorted. The locomotive was classified J83 by the LNER but it had been built for the North British Railway by Neilson, Reid & Co. in March 1901 and was classified D by the NBR. Nineteen other locomotives were produced by the works and a further 20 were constructed at Sharp, Stewart & Co. After Grouping the class were rebuilt with new boilers amongst other changes and, as LNER no. 9810, the locomotive received this attention during September 1924. No. 68457, from September 1948, is at the south end of the shed close to the east side with the turntable discernible to the rear. The locomotive was withdrawn from Haymarket in March 1960.

EDINBURGH HAYMARKET SHED 60530

Heading an express passenger service past its home shed is Peppercorn A2 no. 60530 *Sayajirao*. The locomotive entered traffic from Doncaster Works in March 1948 carrying the number 530 with the 'E' prefix used by BR to denote that the locomotive was of LNER origin. Four Peppercorn A2s (nos. 527-531) were so treated before BR added 60,000 to the class numbering and these numbers were carried from new on subsequently constructed locomotives. *Sayajirao* carried its BR number from November 1948; the last to be changed was no. 529 *Pearl Diver*, which was not altered until September 1949. No. 60530 was initially painted LNER apple green with 'British Railways' applied to the sides of the tender and ran like this until December 1949 when BR Brunswick green with orange and black lining was applied. In January 1950 the engine was reallocated from Peterborough New England shed to Haymarket and it spent the next 11 years working from the depot. The main duty for the A2s at Haymarket was the express passenger service to Aberdeen, usually as far as Dundee. The mechanical coaler seen behind the carriages was installed at the shed in 1930 by Henry Lees & Co. for £15,000 and replaced a coal stage that was in the same position. The coaler was loaded from the southern side and had a capacity of approx. 400 tons, the required amount to be dropped centrally by means of an electrically operated switch. The water tank seen behind the coaler was a more recent fixture being brought into use during the early-1950s replacing a tank (similar in outward appearance to the one at Dalry Road) from the 1890s, which was located on the opposite side of the coaler.

EDINBURGH HAYMARKET SHED 60009

A conventional smokebox door lay behind the front end of the streamlined casing, which was based on a Bugatti-designed petrol railcar. The final design of the front end was arrived at as the result of wind tunnel tests, however, the casing door mechanism had a more humble origin. According to *Locomotives of the LNER Part 2A* by the RCTS, the draughtsman working on the front end was inspired one lunchtime when he observed a dustbin lorry collecting refuse! The locomotive was built at Doncaster Works in June 1937 and was originally numbered 4488; for a brief period before being completed carried the name 'Osprey'. *Union of South Africa* was sent to Haymarket for its first allocation and did not move until May 1962 when relocated to Aberdeen. The engine has been fitted with Automatic Warning System apparatus, the protection plate for it visible behind the drawgear and the cable for it is attached at the front edge of the running plate to the cab. No. 60009 and other A4s at Haymarket had been involved with a forerunner of the system - Hudd Automatic Train Control, which shared similarities with AWS. *Union of South Africa* had the apparatus fitted in July 1939, but after the commencement of the Second World War further development of the system was curtailed and the Hudd equipment had been removed by 1943. No. 60009 was relieved of its duties in June 1966 and later preserved.

Gresley A3 Pacific no. 60035 *Windsor Lad* is seen coming off the turntable at Haymarket after being coaled. In July 1934, as LNER no. 2500, the locomotive was the first of the final nine new A3 locomotives to be constructed. They featured a number of design modifications that included; 5in. diameter steam pipes, perforated steam collectors covered by a 'banjo' dome, sine wave superheater elements and strengthened frames. Apart from a couple of weeks allocated to Aberdeen in March/April 1937, *Windsor Lad* was allocated to Haymarket from new until 1961. In April it spent four months at Carlisle Canal shed before leaving service in September from Haymarket to be quickly scrapped at Doncaster.

EDINBURGH HAYMARKET SHED 68481

Shunting A3 no. 60100 *Spearmint* on the east side of the shed is J83 0-6-0T no. 68481. The locomotive was the final member of the class to be completed and the works responsible was Sharp, Stewart & Co., who released the engine to the NBR in May 1901. The locomotive was renumbered by the LNER in November 1924 to no. 9834 and at the same time was rebuilt by the company. Some other features that were modified during rebuilding included; a significantly smaller dome, Ross pop safety valves in a new position on the firebox, helical springs and increased capacity of the front sandboxes. The new heating surface dimensions were only a slight decrease from what was capable previously. The firebox now had a heating surface of 99.5 sq. ft., a grate area of 16.65 sq. ft. and the total heating surface was 1049.5 sq. ft. The class were mainly employed on shunting duties, however, a Haymarket-allocated example could be found hauling the heavy Corstorphine passenger train for the LNER and later BR. No. 68481 was taken out of service while at Haymarket in February 1962.

EDINBURGH HAYMARKET SHED 60529

After replenishing its coal reserves Peppercorn A2 no. 60529 *Pearl Diver* is reversing on to the turntable to be turned and sent to a shed road in preparation for its next duty. *Pearl Diver* was built at Doncaster in February 1948 to the normal class dimensions, however, when it returned to Doncaster Works for a general repair in July 1949 it was fitted with a double chimney and a M.L.S. multiple valve regulator; four other locomotives were similarly converted around this time. The M.L.S. apparatus consisted of four valves and a pilot valve, which were located in the superheater header and operated by a camshaft; the operating rod from the cab to the header was visible on the right hand side of the locomotive. The double chimney and blastpipe was the Kylchap arrangement first employed on A3 no. 2751 *Humorist* (BR no. 60097) and later the Thompson Pacific Classes, but with clover-shaped orifices instead of taper blocks, which were labour intensive both to produce and maintain. A further difference in the five modified locomotives was the replacement of the perforated steam collector with a tangential steam dryer, which cleaned the steam before it entered the main steam pipe. No other class members were subsequently altered to carry these alterations but the modified engines remained the same throughout their careers. *Pearl Diver*'s career came to an end while at St. Margaret's in December 1962.

EDINBURGH HAYMARKET SHED 60043

No. 60043 *Brown Jack*, the last A3 to be constructed, is waiting at the south end of the shed, perhaps to be allowed on to the turntable, which has presented an opportunity for this scene to be captured. *Brown Jack* left Doncaster Works as LNER no. 2508 in February 1935 to take up its first position at Haymarket. This turned out to be a long-standing residency as the engine did not relocate until November 1961 when switching to St. Margaret's and spending its final two-and-a-half years at the shed, being withdrawn in May 1964. The first shed known as Haymarket was opened on the north side of the E&GR line close to Haymarket station during the early-1840s and was a stone building with two accommodation roads. This building and the site saw a number of extensions and additions over the years that followed, until the capacity of the location was reached by the beginning of the 1890s. It became apparent to the NBR, who had taken over the E&GR in August 1865, that a new shed would be required. A new site was chosen to the west on the approach to Haymarket station, again on the north side of the line. The contract for construction was given to Messrs. James Young & Sons of Edinburgh and a price of £14,500 was agreed with the NBR allowing building work to begin in 1892. However, problems with the ground hampered construction and it was 1894 before the work was finally completed. According to Knox (2011) this was an unacceptable delay for the NBR and they subsequently only paid £13,719 to Messrs. James Young & Sons for the job. The shed had eight tracks covered by a multi-pitched roof supported by brick walls. A 50ft. turntable, coal stage, shear legs, offices and stores were also installed.

EDINBURGH HAYMARKET SHED 60532

The only member of the Peppercorn Pacific Classes to be subsequently preserved was this locomotive - no. 60532 *Blue Peter*. The engine was bought by Geoff Drury during 1968 and restored and then subsequently in the 1980s the locomotive was taken on loan by the North Eastern Locomotive Preservation Group and has worked for them since. It is currently awaiting another overhaul and is on display at Barrow Hill engine shed. *Blue Peter* was built at Doncaster in March 1948 and initially allocated to York before moving to Haymarket in November 1949, which was two months after being fitted with a double chimney and M.L.S valve regulator. In January 1951 the locomotive was swapped allocations with no. 60537 *Bachelors Button*, an Aberdeen resident, as it was noted as a particularly bad performer, which was later attributed to an incorrect blastpipe nozzle setting. No. 60532 worked ten years from Aberdeen and could be at Haymarket shed after completing a service from either there or Dundee as it was stationed at the latter from June 1961. The 70ft. turntable *Blue Peter* is on replaced the 50ft. example in the early 1930s and was produced by Ransomes & Rapier. Before the installation of the larger turntable the Pacifics had to be turned on the local lines. After the war the turntable was changed to vacuum motor operation, which is seen in the foreground and this operated from the engine's vacuum brake pipe. The locomotive was withdrawn in December 1966.

EDINBURGH HAYMARKET SHED 61342

A member of Thompson's B1 Class stands on the turntable during the late-1950s. No. 61342 was erected at Gorton Works in January 1949 and it was (calculated by means of estimation) the 1000th locomotive made at the works. Ten B1s were built at the works and initially they were not given works plates, conforming to the practice at Gorton not to fit them. After the RCTS informed BR that one of the B1s was the holder of this noteworthy milestone they were fitted with works plates, as were locomotives constructed subsequently. No. 61342's first allocation was to Eastfield shed and the main duty for the class working there was the Edinburgh passenger service via both Polmont and Bathgate. Another service saw them on the West Highland Line to Fort William and during the summer holiday periods to Oban. When new the locomotive was fitted with a Stone's steam generator at the front of the running plate for electric lighting equipment, however, this picture seems to show it missing, but the steam supply is still active. No. 61342 has also been fitted with AWS as the protection plate is visible at the front and the battery box is seen below the cab. The engine was withdrawn at the end of December 1966 after moving from Eastfield to Motherwell a month previously.

EDINBURGH HAYMARKET SHED 62743

Another picture illustrating D49 no. 62743 *The Cleveland*. The locomotive fell into class part two as it was fitted with rotary cam operated Lentz poppet valves and 41 other D49s were also fitted with the equipment. Two other class parts existed; part one locomotives were piston valve fitted, while class part three were equipped with Lentz poppet valves that were operated via oscillating cams. Class part three later became extinct when the locomotives were rebuilt with piston valves after the oscillating cams proved unsatisfactory. *The Cleveland* was one of five locomotives to have their axleboxes and bogies altered in the late-1940s to early-1950s because of problems encountered with the riding of the class. Cast steel axleboxes replaced bronze axleboxes and the new bogie they received was similar to that fitted to Thompson's B1 Class. No. 62743 was given these modifications during December 1950 and at this time also received a third mechanical lubricator, seen here in the picture, which was a Wakefield 4-feed type. Haymarket shed closed to steam traffic in September 1963 and then dedicated itself fully to diesel locomotives. Modification of the shed had begun in 1959 when tracks six to eight had been given to the diesel engines, then in 1965 the shed was altered further and the turntable and mechanical coaler were removed from the site. The area remains in use but now as a DMU maintenance depot.

EDINBURGH HAYMARKET SHED 60073

Waiting at the east side of the shed, to join the former Edinburgh & Glasgow Railway line, is Gresley A1 Pacific no. 60073 *St Gatien*. The E&GR began plans for a route between the two cities in the early 1830s, but, this was blocked by Parliament in 1832. In 1835 another connection was proposed and engineering firm Grainger and Miller were employed to plan the route. This line was authorised by an Act of Parliament in July 1838, with construction starting the following year. Edinburgh and Glasgow were connected by 1842 and the line was officially opened on 18 February. As LNER no. 2572, the locomotive was a product of the latter city having been erected by the NBLC during October 1924. *St Gatien* was rebuilt to become a member of the A3 Class between September and November 1945. The engine has been fitted with a double chimney, which was an addition at a general repair that was carried out at Doncaster Works between July and August 1958. The tender, no. 5278, is the Great Northern Railway variety with coal rails that was attached in August 1955. It would appear the wheels have been changed to the disc type, replacing the original 12 spoke type fitted to the tender when built and coupled with LNER no. 2568 *Sceptre*. This alteration probably occurred post-war, but both types of wheels were 4ft. 2in diameter. The tender springs also illustrated here were five inches wide and and were made up of 11 plates; one was ⅝in. thick, while the others were ½in. thick. *St Gatien* was a Heaton resident at this time and had been there since May 1946. The engine made a local switch to Gateshead for the final two months of its working life and was withdrawn in August 1963 to be scrapped at Darlington.

EDINBURGH HAYMARKET SHED 60101

Next to the turntable pit, on no. 1 road at the east end of the shed, is Gresley A3 Pacific no. 60101 *Cicero*. The locomotive was completed at Doncaster Works in June 1930 and was sent to Haymarket along with two other A3s - no. 2975 *Call Boy* and no. 2796 *Spearmint* and both were regulars on the Edinburgh to King's Cross non-stop service. Yet, after the introduction of the A4 Class Pacifics in the late 1930s, *Spearmint* and *Cicero* became nomads for a time, with *Cicero* taking in places such as; Dundee, Glasgow Eastfield and Edinburgh St. Margaret's before returning to Haymarket in October 1940. *Spearmint* had also returned by the end of the year as an attempt was being made to centralise the Scottish A1 and A3 classes for maintenance reasons during the war. *Cicero* remained at Haymarket until January 1963 when it was transferred across the city to St. Margaret's where it saw out the final three months of its career. It was scrapped by Arnott Young, Carmyle.

EDINBURGH HAYMARKET SHED 60098

In the mid-1920s the first Murrayfield stadium was opened to the west of Haymarket shed and one of the stands can be seen behind A3 no. 60098 *Spion Kop*. In the early part of the 1990s the stadium underwent a £50 million redevelopment and the stands would now present and entirely different backdrop. *Spion Kop* was the last of the first order of new A3 Class engines to be completed and was ready for service in April 1929. Before entering traffic the locomotive was fitted experimentally with three different arrangements of cylinder liners and piston rings in an attempt to reduce the high amount of wear occurring to both the cylinders and pistons. The left hand cylinder was fitted with the standard arrangement for the class, while the middle cylinder had mild steel liners and ¾in. cast-iron piston rings. The right hand cylinder also had mild steel liners but with but the piston rings were manufactured from a super nickel alloy. Pistons, for both middle and right hand cylinders, had rims electro-plated with nickel instead of bronze. This experiment appears not to have provided a satisfactory arrangement and an earlier solution was the one finally adopted to solve the problem. In late-1927 the cylinders for no. 2544 *Lemberg*, which had been rebuilt from A1 to A3, were bored to 20½in. and then fitted with cast-iron liners as these were cheap and easy to replace. From 1931 the standard cylinder bore became 21in. and two sizes of cast-iron liners were used for the A1 and A3 classes. Also, in 1928 the pistons began to be made from mild steel in place of the nickel chrome steel type installed previously and the former type were replaced when the need arose. *Spion Kop* was allocated to Doncaster from new until January 1938 when a brief allocation to Haymarket ensued. The locomotive returned to Haymarket in August 1950 and was in residence at the shed until January 1963. Sometime after Nationalisation the locomotive has had the arrangement of the smokebox door handrail altered to be placed above the numberplate, whereas it was usually fitted below it. A number of the class carried this variation but all, apart from no. 60098, reverted to the normal position by 1961. *Spion Kop* was allocated to St. Margaret's for nine months before withdrawal in October 1963 and the locomotive was scrapped at Inverurie Works the following year.

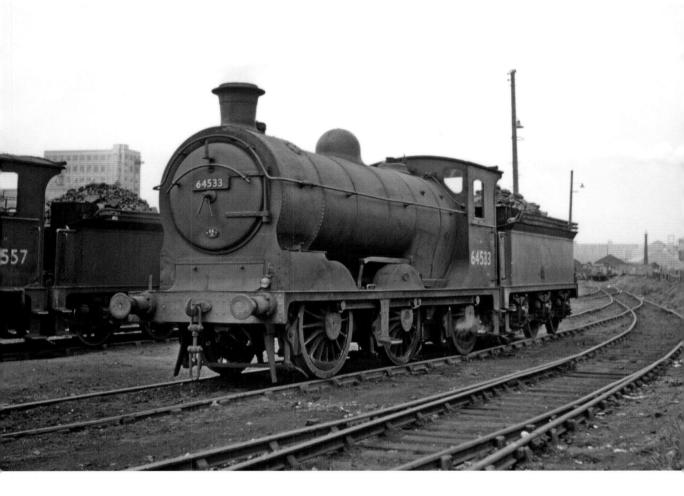

EDINBURGH SOUTH LEITH 64533

The Edinburgh & Dalkeith Railway operated a branch line to Leith from the mid-1830s. This was in addition to their original line between Dalkeith and St. Leonard's, which had been in operation from the beginning of the decade. However, the line was slightly smaller than standard gauge and the traffic was hauled by horses. The line's initial purpose was to transport coal and goods around the city but passenger services were subsequently introduced by the company and proved successful. In the mid-1840s the line was taken over by the NBR and they set about modernising the track, however, when it reopened the passenger numbers dwindled. The passenger services were withdrawn during the 1860s and the line then concentrated on goods traffic. A goods yard at South Leith was put into use to serve the busy docks during the early years of the twentieth century and is still in use; the line leaves the east coast main line at Portobello Junction. Seen in the yard during the late-1950s to early-1960s is J35 Class 0-6-0 no. 64533. The locomotive originally belonged to the NBR B Class designed by W.P Reid. The engines were based on the company's other 0-6-0s, but received larger cylinders (18½in. by 26in.) and a larger boiler (5ft. 4¼in. diameter). No. 64533 entered traffic from Cowlairs Works in March 1913 with slide valves; a number of the earlier examples had piston valves that they retained throughout their careers. The two types were designated J35/3 and J35/1 respectively by the LNER. The company subsequently superheated the class when boiler renewals were necessary and no. 64533, as LNER no. 9126, received the apparatus in July 1927 being then classified J35/4. The locomotive was allocated to St. Margaret's from 1950 until it left service in January 1962. J37 no. 64557 was also at the shed at the same time but left in January 1963 and saw out its career at Dundee Tay Bridge up to October 1963. The building in the background was part of the Scottish Agricultural Industries fertilizer plant.

EDINBURGH ST. MARGARET'S SHED 60089

St. Margaret's shed straddled the east coast main line on the eastern approach to Edinburgh Waverley station. The first building to be erected was a 16 road roundhouse on the north side and this was installed by the NBR during the first half of 1846. On the same side was the company's locomotive construction works, which was active between 1856 and 1869, erecting 33 engines during this period. Subsequently construction duties were transferred to Cowlairs, however, St. Margaret's retained a maintenance function until 1925. A second shed was opened by the NBR, this time on the south side of the line, during 1866 and this contained six tracks that entered the building from the west end. Five years later the NBR added another roundhouse on the south side of the 1866 straight shed for use by the North Eastern Railway, however, it was little used and by the early 1900s the NBR had become the sole occupier. The LNER later demolished this shed to provide space for a 70ft. turntable and sidings, which is where the first new Gresley A3 is pictured. As LNER no. 2743, *Felstead* emerged from Doncaster Works during August 1928 with a diagram 94HP boiler (no. 8075) working at 220lb. per sq. in., 19in. diameter (lined) cylinders and the driver's position switched to the left side of the locomotive. Features of the 94HP boiler included; a reduction in the number of small tubes to 125 of 2¼in. diameter and an increase in the number of superheater flues and elements to 43, which measured 5¼in. and 1¼in. respectively. These changes reduced the total heating surface of the small tubes to be 1398.8 sq. ft. and the new superheater heating surface figures were 1122.8 sq. ft. in the flues and 706 sq. ft in the elements. *Felstead* subsequently carried three new and twelve re-used boilers during its career. Allocation to St. Margaret's was the last for the engine and it arrived in December 1960, staying almost three years, but was withdrawn in October 1963. St. Margaret's survived for a few more years until it was closed by BR in April 1967 and the land was subsequently cleared, providing space for two office blocks that now occupy the southern part of the site.

FORFAR SHED 54489

Seen at the east end of Forfar shed is this example of William Pickersgill's 72 Class of 4-4-0s. The locomotive was completed during March 1921 by Armstrong Whitworth & Co. Ltd and CR no. 84 was applied. As BR no. 54489, it was in traffic until December 1961 and it was later sent for scrap. Pickersgill had worked for the Great Eastern Railway and the Great North of Scotland Railway before joining the CR in 1914 and produced a number of designs for the latter company. He was subsequently employed for a short time by the LMS after grouping until retiring in 1925. This shed was the third building to be erected to house locomotives in Forfar. The first was put in use by the Arbroath and Forfar Railway in March 1839 and it contained a solitary track, but this was closed in 1850 when a four track shed belonging to the CR was opened. In 1848 the company constructed a new station in partnership with the Scottish Midland Junction Railway, which replaced the earlier A&FR station and the increase in traffic necessitated an improved shed. During 1899 a new four road shed was erected to the north of the 1850 shed with a coal stage and 54ft. turntable. The number for the shed in LMS operation was 29D but under BR this was changed to 63C. The shed closed to traffic in July 1964, however, the building still stands but is now surrounded by an industrial estate. Forfar station closed on 4 September 1967 and was demolished during the 1980s.

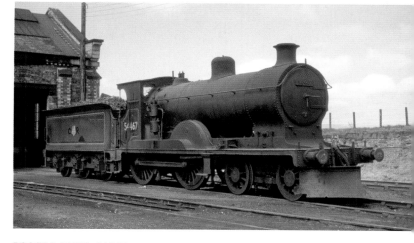

FORFAR SHED 54467

Someone's loyalty obviously lies with the locomotive's pre-Grouping company, the Caledonian Railway, as the initials have been cleaned out of the dirt on the engine's tender. Construction was carried out for the company by the NBLC in March 1916 and the locomotive went to work as CR no. 928. After Grouping the engine became a part of LMS stock and received no. 14467 from them. At Nationalisation the locomotive was allocated to Perth and is seen with its shed code on the smokebox door. No. 54467 did have a spell at Forfar shed between November 1955 and November 1958, but it then returned to Perth to finish its career. The engine, seen at the east end of the shed, was condemned in October 1959.

FORRES SHED 5447I

The shed at Forres was installed by the Inverness & Perth Junction Railway in 1863 and it was built from stone, with the two tracks entering the building from the west end. Other features installed at this time included a turntable, watering facilities and a coal stage. The shed was virtually unaltered throughout its existence and only had wooden gables replace the original stone gables at the beginning of the twentieth century. The shed was passed into Highland Railway hands, then to the LMS before BR took control. The shed code was initially 32C and later changed to 60E. A small number of locomotives were kept at the shed, with nothing larger than a 4-4-0 allocated there; other types included 0-6-0, 0-6-0T and 0-4-4T. No. 54471 had arrived at the shed in July 1954 from Inverness. The locomotive's previous move away from Inverness had been a slightly unusual one to Birkenhead shed in the Liverpool area. It only lasted a few months, however, arriving in July 1953 and returning north to Inverness in October. No. 54471 saw out its career at Forres and was condemned in October 1959. The shed was closed in the late-1950s and was later demolished.

FORRES SHED 55269

The final locomotive to be built in the CR McIntosh 0-4-4T tradition was this engine, no. 55269, which was assembled by Nasmyth Wilson in June 1925. At Nationalisation the locomotive was present at Corkerhill shed and it continued to work from there throughout the 1950s. In January 1959 the engine relocated to Forres, but this was only a brief residency as by May a transfer to Inverness was implemented. This was the final move for the locomotive and three years later it left service to be cut-up.

FORRES SHED 44978

A number of locomotives working in Scotland were fitted with tablet exchange devices, allowing them to work on single lines. The apparatus is visible on the cab side of this Stanier Class Five no. 44978, which is seen outside Forres shed. Two makes of tablet exchangers were used by the LMS and later BR in Scotland - Manson's and Bryson's. A high proportion of the locomotive's fellow classmates resident at Perth shed would have also been similarly equipped.

GALASHIELS SHED 64603

Pictured on Galashiels shed's turntable is LNER Class J37 no. 64603. Located on the west side of the engine shed (seen in the background), the turntable was on a dead-end track that ran to it from the south. The locomotive was originally owned by the NBR and was built for them by the NBLC at their Atlas Works in November 1919. The NBR gave the locomotive the classification 'S' as it had a boiler pressure of 175lb. per sq. in., but this was later increased by 5lb. per sq. in. under orders of the LNER. No. 64603 is coupled with a NBR tender that could hold 3,500 gallons of water and carry seven tons of coal. The locomotive was allocated to St. Margaret's shed for a large proportion of its BR career and only moved during its final year in service. In January 1963 the locomotive found itself at Thornton Junction shed, though it was quickly moved on to Dunfermline and no. 64603 was based there until it was withdrawn in December.

GALASHIELS SHED 62484

Galashiels shed was only a small two road facility built from brick and it was located on the east side of the Waverley line on the southern approach to Galashiels station. The website www.disused-stations.org.uk gives the opening date of the shed as about 1903. Prior to this locomotives had been stabled out in the open on two dedicated tracks. Seen at the shed is LNER D34 'Glen' Class 4-4-0 no. 62484 *Glen Lyon*. The engine previously belonged to the NBR's K Class, which had been brought into being by Matthew Holmes and then locomotives were added by William Reid. All of the class had been built during the first twenty years of the 1900s and different groups had slight variations from the basic design, forming the basis of four LNER classes - D26, D32, D33 and D34. This latter class consisted of 32 locomotives that were erected between 1913 and 1920 and included *Glen Lyon*, which was built at Cowlairs Works in April 1919 as NBR no. 278. The main features of these were their 6ft. diameter driving wheels and superheaters. The Robinson type of superheater was eventually the class standard and it had 22 elements with a heating surface of 192.92 sq. ft. No. 62484 was in service until November 1961. Galashiels shed was closed in April 1962 and used to store locomotives before it was demolished during the 1970s. In 2006 a supermarket was installed on the former site of the shed.

GALASHIELS SHED 64591

Situated approximately 30 miles from Edinburgh, Galashiels station was opened by the NBR during February 1849, but it was not until the end of October that the first phase of the Waverley line as far as Hawick was completed. The station also had goods sidings installed when it was opened and this is probably where the locomotive is photographed. No. 64591 is another LNER J37 Class 0-6-0 and it was built at the same works as no. 64603 but slightly earlier in January 1919. Both locomotives were initially fitted with only one Wakefield mechanical lubricator that was for the engine's two inside cylinders and it was installed in the cab. Others had an additional Wakefield mechanical lubricator for the axles, however, this was placed in the cab and the one for the cylinders was put on the running plate as seen here. The locomotives with only one mechanical lubricator were fitted with a second in the late-1920s and a few members of the class were still to be changed in the 1940s. No. 64591 is seen with the 64A shed code denoting a St. Margaret's shed allocation, although the locomotive could be based at Galashiels shed as the latter was designated a sub-shed of the former and shared shed codes. This allocation lasted between September 1958 and September 1964. The engine was withdrawn from Thornton Junction a month later. Galashiels station closed in January 1969 along with the Waverley line and the track was then lifted. However, reconstruction of part of the line between Edinburgh and Tweedbank is currently underway and at the time of writing is expected to re-open in 2015.

GARELOCHHEAD STATION 67460

Stopped on the 'up' line (now platform two) is a LNER C15 Class 4-4-2T locomotive, which was built for the NBR in August 1912. The design was produced by William Reid and orders for thirty were placed with the Yorkshire Engine Co., who produced the engines between December 1911 and December 1913. The first duties for the class were the suburban passenger services around Glasgow and Edinburgh, but after Grouping the class were gradually dispersed all over Scotland. No. 67460, as LNER no. 9135, was the first member of the class to be fitted with push and pull apparatus to work the West Highland Railway line between Craigendoran and Arrochar. This happened in October 1940 and it was carried on the locomotive until it was one of the final two locomotives to be withdrawn in April 1960. Two other C15s were also fitted with push and pull equipment to provide an alternative to no. 67460 and they were nos. 67474 and 67475. It was acquired by these locomotives in September 1954 and October 1950 respectively. After the locomotives were withdrawn the services were given to a diesel railcar. Since this picture was taken the 'down' line has swapped sides with the 'up' line as part of a reorganisation of station's tracks and the passing loop has been removed.

GARELOCHHEAD STATION 67460

Bill has also captured this picture of no. 67460 arriving at Garelochhead station from the north. The locomotive's last stop would have been Whistlefield station (Whistlefield Halt from 1960), which had been open to passengers since 21 October 1896. Garelochhead station predates it by two years opening with the line on 7 August 1894. Also opened on this date was the locomotive's next stop - Shandon station, which was approximately 3 miles to the south. The line, heading 'down' from Shandon, fell at a gradient of 1 in 68 before returning to the level and then falling again before rising at 1 in 80 as it reaches Garelochhead station. Whistlefield Halt was on the incline to Glen Douglas summit and a 1 in 60 rise would have to be tackled to the station. Both Whistlefield Halt and Shandon station were closed on 15 June 1964. Garelochhead station survives but the station building is now out of use and the windows have been blocked off. It was constructed to a Swiss-style design seen on a number of stations on the line, with brick and timber being the materials used. The island platform the station stands on is accessed from a subway as was the case for many on the West Highland. Measuring approx. 94ft. 6in. long the station contained; a luggage room, a porter's room, stationmaster's office, booking office, waiting room, ladies waiting room, a room for urinals and three toilets.

GEORGEMAS JUNCTION STATION 44978 ◄

Georgemas Junction station was opened on 28 July 1874 by the Sutherland & Caithness Railway. The company's line linked Helmsdale and Wick with a branch at this station for Thurso to the north. A route between the county's two main towns had been mooted in the early 1860s by the Caithness Railway, which gained permission to start work in 1866. However, as the line would be isolated and had no connection to any other railway, capital could not be obtained for construction to commence. In the late-1860s the S&CR was formed by the 3rd Duke of Sutherland to connect his railway between Golspie and Helmsdale with the proposed Caithness Railway line at Georgemas Junction. The Act was passed by Parliament in 1871 and the line was completed at the time of the station's opening. Thomas (1976) noted that funding for the route was contributed by the Highland Railway, £50,000, and the Duke of Sutherland, £60,000. The HR took over the S&CR and the route in July 1884. 'Black Five' no. 44978 is seen at platform one and has been pictured from platform two at Georgemas Junction station. The goods sidings seen behind the locomotive and the platform have since been removed and replaced in 2012 by the Dounreay flask loading facility, which allows waste from the decommissioning of the Dounreay fast reactor research and development facility to be switched from road to rail transport.

GLASGOW BUCHANAN STREET STATION 60026

Towards the end of its career Gresley A4 Pacific no. 60026 *Miles Beevor* was used on the Glasgow - Aberdeen express passenger service and the engine is seen here ready to depart from Glasgow's Buchanan Street Station. The locomotive had arrived in Scotland during October 1963 after being released from its duties at Peterborough New England shed. The allocation was to St. Margaret's but the locomotive was in store at Galashiels until December 1963 and for a time at Bathgate before resuming work and being transferred to Aberdeen Ferryhill in April 1964. Welch (2012) notes some of the scheduled services for A4s at Aberdeen during the summer months of 1965 and they included; 7.10am to Glasgow, 7.45am to Edinburgh (with a return on the 10.30am service to Aberdeen), 5.30pm Glasgow to Aberdeen, 5.30pm Aberdeen to Perth service and 6.30pm Millerhill to Aberdeen freight service. *Miles Beevor* saw 20 months in service from Ferryhill before it was withdrawn in December 1965 and some of its components were used for the preservation of no. 60007 *Sir Nigel Gresley*. Buchanan Street station was opened by the CR on 1 November 1849 after a two mile extension to the site had been built from the existing lines formerly of the Glasgow, Garnkirk & Coatbridge Railway, which had been taken over by the CR in 1846. The extension included a considerable ascent when travelling out of the station with the gradients varying from 1 in 79 and 1 in 98 before the track became relatively level for a distance. In 1932 the station was rebuilt by the LMS, however, the site only remained in use for a further 34 years and it was closed on 7 November 1966, services then moving to Glasgow Queen Street station. The site was cleared during the late-1960s and offices now occupy the land.

CORKERHILL SHED 55225

Ex-CR 439 Class 0-4-4T locomotive no. 55225 is pictured at Corkerhill shed, Glasgow. The bunker of no. 42190, a LMS Fairburn 2-6-4T, is visible to the left of no. 55225. Both were long-term residents at Corkerhill shed, which was located to the west of Corkerhill station and to the south of the line. No. 55225 was resident at the shed from at least Nationalisation until withdrawn in January 1962. No. 42190 worked at the shed between April 1952 and June 1964. No. 55225 has the later BR emblem that has been applied to the locomotive facing the wrong way.

CORKERHILL SHED 55266

Corkerhill shed was on the southern approach to the station of the same name and on the west side of the Paisley Canal line from Glasgow Central. This line was opened in 1885 by the Glasgow & South Western Railway on the former route of the Glasgow, Paisley & Johnstone Canal, which closed in 1881. The locomotive shed was opened by the former company in 1896 and it was a six track facility with entry into it gained from the east and west ends. The tracks, housing approx. 36 engines, were covered by a northlight roof, with a repair shop with one track attached to the north wall. Other provisions included an engine hoist, coal stage with water tank (forming the roof of the stage) and turntable. At the time of the shed's installation, the G&SWR built a 'model' village for the staff at the shed. It was designed by William Melville and contained 136 dwellings of various proportions, which reflected the standing of their occupants in the company. Total cost of the model village came to £70,000. LMS 2P Class locomotive no. 55266 was built by Nasmyth, Wilson & Co. in June 1925 and was in service until September 1961. It is pictured at the shed being stored and the date is probably around the mid-1950s. Corkerhill shed saw some alterations by BR in the late-1940s to early-1950s with a new roof, offices and extension to cover the engine hoist. Steam locomotives were welcome at the shed until May 1967 when it turned its attention to diesel engines. The buildings were then demolished in the 1970s and replaced by a new structure for the stabling of electric locomotives and it has continued in this capacity.

CORKERHILL SHED 45707

At the south end of Corkerhill shed and in front of the LMS No. 1 type mechanical coal stage is LMS Stanier 'Jubilee' Class 4-6-0 no. 45707 *Valiant*. The locomotive was constructed at Crewe in May 1936 at an approximate cost of £6,330. From LMS no. 5702 the class were built with an altered superheater arrangement as the one previously fitted to the locomotives was inadequate. The engines were fitted with 159 small tubes and 24 superheater elements that were 1¼ diameter. The superheater heating surface was thus increased to 307 square feet. When entering service *Valiant* was paired with a tender taken from 'Royal Scot' Class locomotive LMS no. 6140 *The King's Royal Rifle Corps*, no. 3936, while tender no. 9341 was attached to the latter locomotive. No. 45707 had three spells at Corkerhill; August 1954 to October 1957, April 1958 to November 1959 and April 1960 to withdrawal in December 1962. From Corkerhill, the locomotive's duties included services to Leeds, Bradford and Stranraer. *Valiant* spent much of its final year stored at the shed and its date of withdrawal also saw the remaining Jubilees in Scotland leave service in the country.

DAWSHOLM SHED GWR 3440

A long way from its native metals is Great Western Railway locomotive no. 3440 *City of Truro*, which has been photographed at Dawsholm shed, Glasgow. The locomotive was the two thousandth to be erected at Swindon Works in 1903 and it entered the company's 3700 Class (alternatively known as the City Class) of 4-4-0s. A total of twenty members of this class were produced between 1902 and 1909 to the design of George Churchward (CME of the GWR from 1902 to 1922). The locomotives featured taper boilers with a Belpaire firebox, two inside cylinders that were 18in. diameter by 26in. stroke and they had 6ft. 8½in. diameter driving wheels. *City of Truro* was in service until March 1931 and was subsequently donated to the LNER's museum at York where it resided until restored by BR in 1958. It was withdrawn again in 1961 this time going to the GWR museum for static display. Another return to steam came in 1984 and the locomotive has been in and out of service since this time but is currently operational and owned by the National Railway Museum.

DAWSHOLM SHED 57245

Seen on one of the two repair shop roads at the shed is no. 57245, a CR Drummond 'Jumbo' goods 0-6-0 locomotive. The repair shop at Dawsholm was located on the west side of the shed and was equipped with a 40 ton engine lift, a smiths shop and mess room adjoined to the rear. Drummond took over the role of CR Locomotive Superintendent in 1882 from George Brittain. Design work for the 'Jumbos' started in October of that year and progressed steadily into 1883. After his appointment Drummond sought to improve and expand St Rollox Works, consequently it was unavailable for construction of new locomotives, so independent contractors were required and Neilson & Co. (Neilson, Reid & Co. from 1898) were eventually chosen. They produced 15 goods engines as well as 10 passenger locomotives and charged the CR £72,500. As CR no. 307, the engine was ready for service in December 1883. Two features of the locomotives produced Neilson & Co. were the provision of 2,500 gallon tenders and iron crank axles. No. 57245 was allocated to Dawsholm from April 1941 and possibly did not move away before it left service in September 1961.

DAWSHOLM SHED 57470

Pictured in storage next to Dawsholm shed's coal stage is a former CR McIntosh 711 Class 0-6-0 locomotive. The design was originated by Drummond in the early 1880s and was replicated by successive Locomotive Superintendents until the end of the 19th century. This example was constructed at St Rollox Works in February 1897 as part of order Y47 for five engines. The cost of these locomotives, given by Cornwell (2011), was £2,001. After Grouping the locomotive was stripped of its CR number, 584, and given LMS no. 17470. No. 57470 was a long-term Dawsholm resident and was taken out of work from the shed during September 1961 and was later scrapped.

DAWSHOLM SHED 56039

Another locomotive being stored at Dawsholm is this Caledonian Railway 'Pug' engine. Again, the plans for the class were introduced by Drummond in the early 1880s. No. 56039 is a later example that was produced under the direction of McIntosh as part of the 611 Class of 0-4-0ST; earlier locomotives were part of the 264 Class. St Rollox Works erected it in December 1908 and it was allocated CR no. 463; it was the last of 40 of the type produced for the CR. At Grouping LMS no. 16039 was given to the engine and the classes were designated 0F by the company. At the formation of BR the locomotive was allocated to the shed but by early-1950 had found its way to Yoker. Staying there until February 1961, it had a number of spells loaned to industrial locations in the area such as; B&W Ltd., Renfrew, between December 1950 and January 1951 as well as the Ministry of Supply, Paisley between September and November 1950. It was in service at Dawsholm until withdrawn in October 1962.

DAWSHOLM SHED 69511

Illustrated here is a Great Northern Railway N2 Class (LNER N2) 0-6-2T locomotive built by the North British Locomotive Company in January 1921. H.N. Gresley produced the design and it was based on his predecessor's (H.A. Ivatt) N1 Class locomotives. However, they featured a number of differences including; superheater, increased diameter cylinders with piston valves and greater boiler pitch. Sixty were produced for the GNR; ten at Doncaster Works and 50 by the NBLC and all were fitted with condensing apparatus so they could work the London Metropolitan lines. These caused problems with water surge and underwent a number of modifications in an attempt to eradicate the problem, which was never fully resolved. No. 69511 had its condenser removed in March 1928, in all likelihood when it was transferred to Scotland along with a number of other N2's. Also at this time the locomotive was equipped with Westinghouse brake pumps in addition to its originally fitted vacuum brakes, however, the Westinghouse apparatus was removed in November 1945. The locomotive arrived at Dawsholm from Parkhead shed in May 1952 and stayed to be condemned in December 1960.

DAWSHOLM SHED 56336

This locomotive belonged to CR Class 782 and was built at St Rollox Works in November 1910. It had 4ft. 6in. diameter driving wheels, two inside cylinders of 18 in. diameter by 26in. stroke and a boiler pressure of 160psi. The locomotive was allocated to Dawsholm between June 1958 and June 1962 and had previously spent a number of years at Grangemouth shed. It had a further six months at work allocated to Motherwell before it was sent to be scrapped in December 1962.

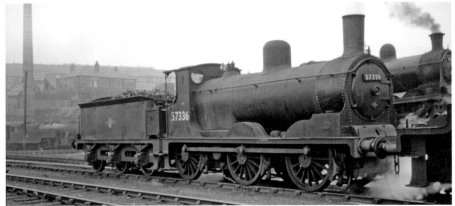

DAWSHOLM SHED 57336

Dawsholm shed was opened in 1896 by the Caledonian Railway at an approximate cost of £7,931; construction was carried out by Robert McAlpine. The shed had six tracks, a northlight roof, coal stage and 50ft. turntable; the latter two present on the west side of the site. This CR 'Jumbo' was built at St Rollox Works in July 1892. At the time of this photograph the engine was based at Hurlford, but was only there six months between June and December 1962. The locomotive had been allocated to Dawsholm previously and had moved to Hamilton. The final move for no. 57336 was to Ardrossan before it ceased to be in service from September 1963. The shed closed on 3 October 1964 and the site is now occupied by residential properties.

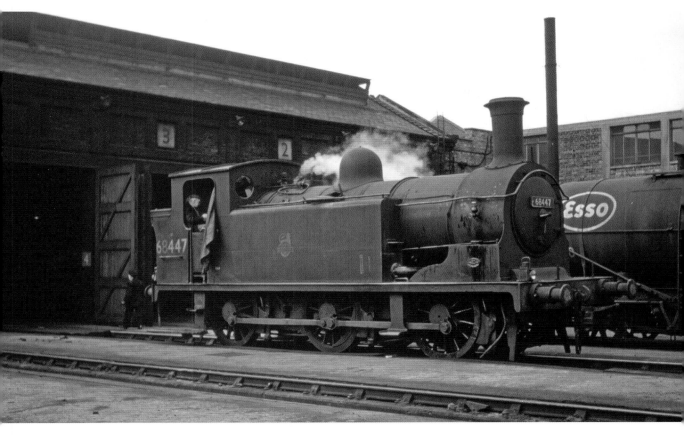

GLASGOW EASTFIELD SHED 68447

Emerging from no. 4 road at Glasgow Eastfield shed is J83 Class 0-6-0T no. 68447, which was constructed by Neilson, Reid & Co. in September 1900. The locomotive was rebuilt by the LNER in May 1924 and at the same time received no. 9800 from the company. In March 1946 the locomotive received no. 8447 as part of the complete renumbering of LNER locomotives and the class were dealt with between January and June 1946. The engine's BR no. was acquired during August 1948 and at this time the locomotive was allocated to Eastfield shed and was still there when withdrawn in February 1961.

GLASGOW EASTFIELD SHED 64562

A 'foreign' J37 0-6-0 is pictured at Eastfield probably in preparation for a return to its home shed - Edinburgh St. Margaret's. No. 64562 was built by the NBLC's Atlas Works in July 1918 and went into service as NBR no. 158. The NBLC constructed 79 J37 engines between 1918 and 1921, with Cowlairs the other works responsible for constructing the remaining 25 members of the class. In the late-1950s the class began to be fitted with AWS apparatus and no. 64562 was one of thirty to be fitted with it. Interestingly, they were the only former NBR locomotives to be fitted with AWS. The locomotive was based at St. Margaret's throughout its career under BR and was in service until November 1963.

GLASGOW EASTFIELD SHED
69171

Located on the east side of the former Edinburgh & Glasgow Railway line, the shed at Eastfield was opened during September 1904 for the NBR. The shed contained 14 roads making it the largest facility operated by the company. In 1919 the shed was destroyed by fire but was subsequently rebuilt and at Grouping the shed passed to LNER ownership. Sometime later, the LNER installed a mechanical coaling plant at the site, which replaced a ramped coal stage that had been installed when the shed was first built. N15/1 Class 0-6-2T engine no. 69171 was erected by the NBLC's Queens Park Works in May 1913 and was the last of a batch of nine to be completed during the month. The locomotive was allocated to Parkhead at Nationalisation and left there in April 1954 to take up its new position at Eastfield. Withdrawal from the shed came in June 1960. The shed closed to steam in November 1966 and the land was re-utilised as a diesel depot, which remained its role until closed in 1992. The site was then cleared, however, in 2004 the site was given a new role as DMU traincare facility.

GLASGOW EASTFIELD SHED 69218

Another N15/1, this time a post-grouping addition to the class, has been photographed by Bill at Eastfield shed. No. 69218 was erected at Cowlairs Works in February 1924 and given no. 79 with a 'B' suffix. After Grouping duplicates of locomotive's numbers occurred with up to seven engines carrying the same number and it took a while before a satisfactory solution was devised. The first attempt saw a suffix added to the locomotive's number depending on which works the engines were built at; Cowlairs was designated with a 'B suffix. However, duplicates still existed within this system, including a number of the N15 Class, who shared numbers with members of the Great Central Railway's J58 Class of 0-6-0s. The 1924 renumbering scheme was then conceived where x000 would be added to the numbers depending on the constituent company. The NBR's designated number was 9000 and this was added to the N15 numbers between 1924 and 1926; no. 79B had LNER no. 9079 applied in June 1926. No. 69218 was at Carlisle Canal shed in 1948 and moved over the border to Glasgow in September 1951. Its stay at Eastfield was only broken by a three month spell at Dawsholm between August and November 1961. The locomotive left service in October 1962.

GLASGOW EASTFIELD SHED 68336

On the east side of the site, at the shed's ash pits, is a J88 Class 0-6-0T, which has been pictured next to an unidentified Stanier 'Black Five'. No. 68336 entered traffic for the NBR from Cowlairs Works in April 1909 after being built to Reid's Class F design. Some features of this were; two cylinders measuring 15in. diameter by 22in. stroke, Stephenson motion with slide valves, a 3ft. 10in. diameter boiler that was 8ft. 8½in. long, 3ft. 9in. diameter wheels, total heating surface of 651.2 sq. ft., water capacity of 850 gallons and space for just over 2 tons of coal. The engine resided at Eastfield during the late-1940s to early-1950s before it transferred to Kipps in May 1954, staying six years at the shed. The next move to Dawsholm was the final one for no. 68336 and it took place during October 1960. It was condemned in May 1962.

GLASGOW EASTFIELD SHED 68468

Standing next to Eastfield's water tank is J83 no. 68468. What appears to be a carriage body can be seen on the extreme right, while the mechanical coaler is just showing its top above the tank. No. 68468 was manufactured by Sharp, Stewart & Co. in April 1901 and was subsequently rebuilt by the LNER in September 1924. The engine was one of several members of the class to be fitted with drop grates during the late-1930s and received the alteration, as no. 9821, in January 1936. The tank had to be modified to allow the fitting of the equipment and this resulted in a slight decrease of the 800 gallons that could be carried by the locomotive. No. 68468 was at Eastfield from Nationalisation until withdrawn in June 1959. Seven of the J83 Class were at Eastfield during the 1950s and the duties for the class at the shed would have included shunting and pilot work.

GLASGOW EASTFIELD SHED 67644

No. 67600, seen on the left at the shed's ash pits, was the first of the class to be built, emerging from Doncaster Works in September 1930, while no. 67644 was erected at the works a few years later in August 1935. Both were designated V3 and the first to be changed was no. 67600 during March 1956, with no. 67644 following in July 1958. The locomotives were long-term residents at Eastfield during the BR period but no. 67600 had been there since entering traffic and had only spent two months allocated away. No. 67644 started its career at Heaton shed before being transferred to Scotland in 1939/1940 and had been at Dunfermline at Nationalisation before reaching Eastfield. The V1s at the shed could be used on suburban passenger traffic, goods and coast services. One particular duty, that no. 67600 has been fitted with a slip coupling for, was banking trains out of Queen Street station as a steep incline was present. Part of the slip coupling equipment can be just seen protruding from the locomotive's smokebox and several other engines in the V1 Class were similarly equipped from the same task. Despite being the older engine no. 67600 survived in service until December 1962, while no. 67644 had been sent to be scrapped in May 1962.

◆ GLASGOW EASTFIELD SHED 62496

A Gresley V1 2-6-2T and a D34 Class 4-4-0 stand together on no. 1 and no. 2 roads at Eastfield. The two locomotives could have been closely related in terms of boiler specifications as it was originally proposed that the V1 Class should carry a boiler based on that carried by the D34 Class, however, this idea was subsequently dropped. No. 67629 was erected at Doncaster Works in February 1935 and was one of only 18 not to be modified to be reclassified V3. The engine was a Parkhead shed resident at the time of this picture and it had been there since moving from St. Margaret's in January 1959; it left service while at the shed in May 1962. No. 62496 *Glen Loy* was 15 years older than the V1 having been constructed at Cowlairs Works in August 1920. Like the V1, *Glen Loy* was also little altered from when it was built and so were the rest of the D34 Class. One minor modification the locomotive received, as LNER no. 9494, was a drop grate that was fitted in June 1934; other members of the class were also altered around this time. A class-wide change was the removal of Westinghouse brake equipment, which was then replaced with steam brakes; *Glen Loy* was given them in July 1936. Under BR the locomotive was only allocated to Eastfield as were a few other D34s. The shed had a long association with the class and 13 were at Eastfield during the early 1950s for local passenger services. For the LNER, the locomotives would have worked passenger services further afield to Edinburgh, Dundee and Perth and were particularly noted on the West Highland line where they were well suited to the nature of the track. *Glen Loy* was withdrawn in November 1961.

GLASGOW PARKHEAD SHED 62672

LNER D11/2 'Director' 4-4-0 no. 62672 *Baron of Bradwardine* was constructed after Grouping and based on the design for Robinson's 11F Class, which were built for the Great Central Railway. Twenty-four were constructed during 1924 for work in Scotland as there was a shortage of engines suitable for express passenger work on former NBR lines. Two works were employed for the construction of these locomotives – Kitson & Co. and Armstrong Whitworth & Co. Ltd, with the work split equally between them. No. 62672, as LNER no. 6379 emerged as the second engine to be completed from Kitson & Co. in August 1924. The locomotives built for the LNER had a number of differences from the 11 constructed for the GCR (classified D11/1) including; cab height reduction, shorter boiler mounts and water scoops were omitted from the tender. The first two changes mentioned above were applied to allow the locomotives to conform to the NBR load gauge, which was not as generous as it was on the GCR. There were also no water troughs on the former NBR lines negating the need for water scoops. The locomotive's name was applied in April 1925 and the valances that were originally fitted below it, to the running plate, were dispensed with in February 1926. *Baron of Bradwardine* was allocated to Eastfield from new and between 1933 and 1935 the engine was fitted with a drop grate as a result of the installation of a wet ash pit there. During the early days of its time in service from Eastfield the locomotive was employed mainly on express passenger duties between Glasgow and Edinburgh. However, after the Second World War the class were displaced to secondary passenger services and from the mid-1950s many found themselves unemployed and in storage at various locations. No. 62672 was withdrawn from Eastfield in September 1961.

GLASGOW PARKHEAD SHED 69209

This post-Grouping N15/1 0-6-2T locomotive, no. 69209, was built at Cowlairs Works in November 1923 and has been photographed at Glasgow Parkhead shed's ash pits. The engines built after 1923 had diagram 81 boilers that were virtually the same as the NBR boilers, but they were equipped with Ross pop safety valves on the firebox. A cab ventilator was also an additional item for the later locomotives and a few of the earlier engines later received them; it is visible here on the cab roof. Shunting footsteps are fitted to no. 69209, along with a handrail on the bunker and this would have been present when it entered traffic. It would have been a standard fixture on engines produced from 1916, while some of the class that had been built before this date latterly acquired them. No. 69209 was based at Burnbank, a sub-shed of Parkhead for a time during the late-1920s to early-1930s before the former closed and nine other N15s could also have been found there for local coal traffic. At Parkhead goods and pilot duties were the mainstay of the class and in 1950 nineteen N15s were allocated to Parkhead. No. 69209 was a long-term resident and its time in service was discontinued during October 1960.

GLASGOW POLMADIE SHED 46227

Two views of LMS Stanier Coronation Pacific no. 46227 *Duchess of Devonshire* are included here, which see it being turned on Polmadie shed's turntable. This was located on the northern perimeter a distance away from the shed building, but quite close to the mechanical coaler and judging from the tender the latter appears to have been recently visited. Installed when the shed opened, the first turntable was 51ft. diameter and located at the rear of the engine shed. A 70ft. example from Cowans Sheldon replaced the earlier turntable on the same site in 1934, but in the mid-1940s a second 70ft. turntable supplanted this at the location seen here. The move was the result of a rationalisation of the facilities at the shed during the early-1940s as the previous location had been more convenient for engines working in the nearby goods and mineral yards, rather than the locomotives allocated to the shed. No. 46227 was built at Crewe Works in June 1938 as part of a batch of 10 authorised under the 1938 building programme and were estimated to cost £138,000. This engine cost £9,732 to manufacture, with the tender costing an additional £1,570. Five of the 1938-built Coronation Class were streamlined while the other five were built without; *Duchess of Devonshire* had it fitted when entering traffic. The first of the class to have it removed was LMS no. 6235 *City of Birmingham* with the others following suit in the ensuing years; no. 46227 had the streamlining removed in August 1946. A number of features seen on the locomotive were added after construction, such as the double chimney fitted in December 1940 and the smoke deflectors that were carried from February 1947. The smokebox reverted to a normal appearance in October 1952 after originally being tapered to accommodate the streamlined casing. Prior to Nationalisation the locomotive had been allocated to English sheds but in June 1948 *Duchess of Devonshire* moved from Crewe North to Polmadie and operated from the shed until withdrawn in December 1962. The locomotive was scrapped at Crewe Works in November 1963.

GLASGOW POLMADIE SHED 55237

This former Caledonian Railway locomotive belonged to a small class of only four engines when it entered service in August 1922. It was the first of the CR 431 Class of 0-4-4T to be built for banking duties and for this they featured cast-iron buffer beams. The locomotive started its career as CR no. 431, later becoming LMS no. 15237 and classified 2P by the company. At Nationalisation the locomotive resided at Beattock and in July 1955 was transferred to Polmadie. The locomotive has been photographed at the rear of the shed roughly on the site of the old turntable before it was moved to a position seen in the pictures of no. 46227 *Duchess of Devonshire*. No. 55237 moved to Oban in December 1960 and was later withdrawn from the shed in July 1961. The CR 431 class had become extinct by the end of the year.

GLASGOW POLMADIE SHED 80003

A smart-looking BR Standard Class 4 2-6-4T locomotive is pictured in Polmadie shed yard. The class were built to replace life expired tender and tank locomotives on local passenger services, with the inspiration for the design coming from the LMS Fairburn 2-6-4T. A number of modifications were made though and these included; altered frames, increased boiler pressure, shorter bogie wheelbase and reduced total length. The first members of the class were included in BR's 1951 building programme and no. 80003 emerged from Derby Works along with nine others, with a further 44 scheduled to be built at Brighton Works. In the event the order at Derby Works was delayed and the first locomotive did not appear until September 1952 with no. 80003 following in October. In *British Railways Standard Steam Locomotives Volume Three* (2007) the official cost of these engines is given as £15,453, which is broken down into £14,643 for construction, £522 for other costs and £288 for capital interest. These ten locomotives from Derby were destined for the Scottish Region and they were split between Ayr, Polmadie, Motherwell, Kittybrewster and Corkerhill. No. 80003 was initially allocated to Motherwell, however, by November 1952 the engine had been transferred to Polmadie; the locomotive at Ayr was also quickly moved and sent to Corkerhill. A number of the class worked from Polmadie during their existence and they could be found on suburban services, to the Clyde coast and to Edinburgh via Shotts. No. 80003 left for St. Margaret's in June 1962 and was withdrawn from there in March 1965.

GLASGOW POLMADIE SHED 57292

Flanked by two diesel shunting engines in Polmadie shed's yard is a CR Drummond 'Jumbo' 0-6-0, no. 57292. The locomotive was manufactured in September 1886 at St Rollox Works as CR no. 318, but by Grouping the number had become CR no. 1318. The engine was built in the third order for the design placed at St Rollox after the works had been upgraded. These locomotives reverted to the use of iron for the crankaxles, which replaced steel used for the previous two batches, but retained features such as the cylinder arrangement and capacity of the tender. As no. 318 the locomotive was rebuilt by the CR in 1910, receiving a new pattern boiler, but keeping its original frames, which were replaced on some of the class that were rebuilt at this time. In 1917 the locomotive was given to the Railway Operating Division for use in France during the First World War along with 24 other CR 'Jumbo' 0-6-0s from the various designers. The engine was returned in 1919, resulting in the renumbering mentioned earlier, as the CR had removed the 25 from the company's locomotive register. From at least 1948 until it left service in December 1961, no. 57292 was allocated to Polmadie. Nine diesel shunters worked at the shed from 1956.

GLASGOW POLMADIE SHED 72000

Of the 999 Standard Class locomotives built for BR between 1951 and 1960, sixty-six featured a 4-6-2 wheel arrangement. Ten of these were erected to the Standard Class 6 or 'Clan' design and they emerged from Crewe Works after the first 25 Standard Class 7s had been completed. The Standard Class 6 Pacifics had been two years on the drawing board after authorisation had been given in 1949 for the design work to begin at Derby drawing office. The 'Britannia' and 'Clan' locomotives were different among the Standard Classes as they had a new design of boiler and a wide firebox and they were not derivative as some of the other Standard Class features were. The boiler and firebox construction did have some roots in LMS practice, however, as R.A. Riddles, R.C. Bond and E.S. Cox were part of the design team. The two classes also shared the same frames and motion, but differences included boiler, firebox and cylinder dimensions. Some of these were, on the 'Clans' and 'Britannias' respectively; 6ft. 1in. diameter boiler - 6ft. 5in.; firebox heating surface of 195 sq. ft. - 210 sq. ft.; cylinders of 19½in. by 28in. - 20in. by 28in. No. 72000 *Clan Buchanan* was one of five members of the class to reside at Polmadie over two and three spells during their time in service.

GLASGOW POLMADIE SHED D5708

British Railways Class 28 diesel-electric locomotive no. D5708 is pictured with another (unidentified) member of the class as they usually worked in pairs using the Red Circle Coupling System. D5708 was built by Metropolitan-Vickers at their Bowesfield Works in January 1959 as part of a pilot order for 20 from BR. The design was unusual as it utilised a Co-Bo wheel arrangement (a six wheel and a four wheel bogie). The engine used was a Crossley HSTV8 2-stroke, which developed 1,200hp and a Metropolitan-Vickers traction motor was also employed. D5708 was allocated to Derby shed from new until moved to Barrow-in-Furness in February 1962 and was later based at either of the Carlisle sheds. From their home depot the class could be employed on freight and local passenger services. As with other BR diesel classes at the time the Class 28s were beset by problems and saw early withdrawal. D5708 left service in September 1968 and was scrapped, while the last of the class went to the breakers yard the following year. D5705 has been preserved.

GLASGOW POLMADIE SHED 45542

A visitor from Preston shed, no. 45542 appears to have had its smokebox cleaned recently, with remnants of the task visible below the smokebox door. The engine was part of the Patriot Class of locomotives that were introduced by LMS CME Sir Henry Fowler in 1930. No. 45542 was built at Crewe Works in March 1934 as the first of the final ten made to the design; forty-two had been nominally rebuilt from Claughton Class 4-6-0s in the preceding years. Many members of the class were named, however, seven remained without including no. 45542. At Nationalisation the locomotive was allocated to Crewe North but by September 1950 it had reached Carlisle Upperby, which welcomed 33 Patriots during the BR period. In November 1958 the engine moved south to Preston and then in July 1961 ventured even further south to Nuneaton. No. 45542 left service in June 1962.

GLASGOW POLMADIE SHED 46156

Entering traffic from Derby Works in October 1930 as LMS no. 6156, the locomotive was not named *The South Wales Borderer* until the following October. During the first few years in service the class experienced a number of problems, one of them being smoke drifting to the cab in a way detrimental to the driver's vision. A number of attempts to solve the problem resulted in straight deflector plates being fitted at either side of the smokebox and no. 6156 received the plates in January 1932. As BR no. 46156 the engine was rebuilt in May 1954 and received the type of smoke deflectors seen here a month later. The smokebox is displaying the 8A shed code, which means that it was based at Edge Hill shed at the time of the photograph. *The South Wales Borderer* was assigned to the shed from June 1958 to November 1959 but had been there previously while working for the LMS and this stay lasted from November 1946 to January 1953. Crewe North was a frequent home for the locomotive as it notched up eight allocations during its lifetime, while other places frequently visited included Holyhead (5) and Longsight (4). The final move was from Willesden to Annesley in October 1963 and the locomotive was subsequently withdrawn in October 1964. No. 46156 was scrapped by A. Draper, Hull, during 1965.

GLASGOW POLMADIE SHED 70051

Taken during April 1957 this image of Standard Class 7 Pacific no. 70051 *Firth of Forth* shows the engine at the shed's ash pits. The late-1940s saw the modernisation of certain facilities at Polmadie and one of note was the ash disposal plant, which was the first of its type in Britain. Four 190ft. long ash pits were located near the mechanical coaler and they had grids on the floor of the pit allowing ash to fall into concrete hoppers. The ash was then directed onto one of two conveyor belts that were submerged in water and which then transported it to a belt that ran across the end of the pits. Operable at three speeds, this belt led the detritus to another belt that was inclined to run up to the 50ft. high concrete silo that could store 50 tons of the waste. The ash could then be deposited into empty coal wagons and transported for disposal. Polmadie saw relatively few members of the class, apart from those initially allocated, and only three of these were present for work into the 1960s. All had left by April 1962.

GLASGOW POLMADIE SHED 72004

No. 72004 *Clan MacDonald* went into service during February 1952 and had cost £21,283 to complete. The locomotive was at Polmadie for the bulk of its life with only a four month spell at St. Margaret's breaking this up. *Clan MacDonald* was withdrawn at the end of December 1962 after only accumulating approx. 36,000 miles since its last major works visit. Darlington Works were eventually given the task of dismantling the locomotive but this was not completed until the early part of 1964.

GLASGOW POLMADIE SHED 56239

The CR desired further accommodation for locomotives in the south of Glasgow and they chose a site on the north side of the line to Carstairs just before Rutherglen station. By 30 December 1873 a quote for £12,750 was chosen, allowing the construction of the shed to begin. Polmadie was operational sometime during 1875 and it contained 14 roads with a two track repair shop located on the north side. As with a number of other sheds, timber was the surprising choice for the material to be used and before long the whole shed required replacement. At Grouping the LMS took over Polmadie shed and almost immediately set in motion plans to rebuild the depot. Construction then proceeded at an estimated cost of £112,000. The new shed had similar proportions to the old shed, but this time it was constructed using bricks. The repair shop was also upgraded at this time acquiring a pair of 35 ton cranes and the machine shop was also renewed. Two 20,000 gallon water tanks were also installed on the site along with a 400 ton capacity mechanical coaler, which could hold three grades of coal for the different duties held at the shed. This former CR McIntosh locomotive, no. 56239, is seen on a repair shop road sometime in the late-1950s to early-1960s. It had been built at St Rollox Works in December 1895 and was active until March 1961; under BR no. 56239 had been allocated to Polmadie. The shed closed to steam in May 1967 and then housed diesel locomotives, however, these are no longer based at the facility. The shed has subsequently been demolished but the repair shop is still in use.

GLASGOW QUEEN STREET STATION 69181 AND 67671

Glasgow Queen Street station was brought into being by the Edinburgh & Glasgow Railway and was opened on 21 February 1842. Trains leaving the station have to negotiate a 1 in 45 climb through a 1,006 yard tunnel and onto Cowlairs Junction, with some trains in former times requiring assistance from a banking engine. Nos. 69181 and 67671 are possibly on standby for this duty or could be waiting to start a passenger service. No. 69181 was built by the NBLC in February 1918 and entered NBR Class A. The locomotive was fitted with steam brakes originally and these were later augmented by a vacuum ejector that was fitted in March 1948. This modification was given to engines working in Edinburgh goods yards and those working at Queen Street station. The locomotive was based at Eastfield and was removed from its duties while there in February 1962. No. 67671, a LNER V1 Class locomotive, was built at Doncaster Works in October 1938 and was not subsequently reclassified V3. The engine was fitted with Westinghouse and vacuum brakes when new to work suburban services out of London Liverpool Street station, but the Westinghouse apparatus was later removed in March 1954. The locomotive left service in July 1960.

GLASGOW ST ROLLOX SHED 54474

A CR Pickersgill Class 113 4-4-0 is seen in a decrepit state at the side of St Rollox shed. The locomotive was constructed by the NBLC in July 1916 and was one of 16 produced to the design. Class members nos. 54474 and 54475 were present at the shed for Nationalisation and resided there until withdrawn in October 1959 and June 1961 respectively. Nos. 54472 and 54473 joined them briefly in July 1959.

◆ GLASGOW ST ROLLOX SHED 60034

Lord Faringdon was the 35th and final A4 Pacific to be constructed and left Doncaster Works in July 1938 as LNER no. 4903. Initially, the locomotive was named *Peregrine* following 24 other members of the class being named after birds. Renaming to *Lord Faringdon* was also the final renaming of an A4 locomotive when it changed in March 1948; twelve other A4s had a name change while in service with ten of these carrying the names of the upper hierarchy of the LNER. Lord Faringdon had been Chairman of the Great Central Railway from 1899 until Grouping, then taking on the position of Deputy Chairman of the LNER; a post that he held until his death in March 1934. Three locomotives had previously carried his name before this A4. The first was GCR Class 11B (LNER Class D9) no. 1014 *Sir Alexander* then GCR Class 11E (LNER Class D10) no. 429 *Sir Alexander Henderson*. GCR Class 9P (LNER Class B3) no. 1169 then carried *Lord Faringdon*, denoting his peerage, until the locomotive was withdrawn in December 1947. No. 60034 was one of four that entered traffic with a double blastpipe and Kylchap cowls. The blastpipe orifice was 5in., with the area of the blast nozzle standing at 29.9 sq. in. and no. 3 taper blocks were fitted. In the April after Nationalisation the locomotive began a prolonged residency at King's Cross shed, only moving to Peterborough New England when the former closed to steam in June 1963. *Lord Faringdon* was then sent to St. Margaret's in October and subsequently put in store at Galashiels and Bathgate before arriving at Aberdeen in May 1964 to re-start its career. St Rollox shed did have two A4s on hand for services to Aberdeen for a time - no. 60027 *Merlin* and no. 60031 *Golden Plover*. No. 60034 *Lord Faringdon* ceased its duties in August 1966 and it was then sent to be scrapped. The shed was virtually unaltered from when built at the time of its closure in November 1966 and after demolition the site has been left to nature.

GLASGOW ST ROLLOX SHED 73154

No. 73154, a BR Standard Class 5 4-6-0, entered traffic in June 1957 from Derby Works with British-Caprotti valve gear. The locomotive was one of ten so fitted that were sent to Scotland and allocated to St Rollox shed. The engines fitted with British-Caprotti valve gear cost BR £28,075 compared to the Walschaerts valve gear fitted locomotives that, during 1957, cost £22,606 to produce. From St Rollox the class were regulars on services from Glasgow Buchanan Street station to places such as Dundee and Aberdeen; with the 6.15pm Dundee to Glasgow fish train usually handled by a member of the class after completing a passenger service to Dundee. Several types of tender were fitted to the Standard Class 5s and the type received depended on the allocation and the intended duties. No. 73154 was originally fitted with a BR1B tender with straight sides, which had increased water capacity over the BR1 tender to 4,725 gallons and coal capacity of 7 tons. After experience gained of the latter tender in service the BR1B design was changed to include a fall plate and gangway doors as the footplate proved to be a rather draughty place without them. The locomotive left service from Motherwell in December 1966; six months short of being ten years old.

GLASGOW ST ROLLOX SHED 60007

While modernisation of the railways continued apace so did the improvement of cities' housing up and down Britain. Rising behind St Rollox shed (also known as Balornock) is Tower 7, 153-213 Petershill Drive, of the Red Road housing development. Eight blocks were built between 1964 and 1969 to house 4,700 people and to two types of design. Tower 7 was 28 storeys high and one of two of the wider 'slab' design, while the other six were 31 storeys and of the more traditional tower block design. Tower 7 had the distinction of being the first to be demolished in mid-2012 and the rest of the housing estate is to follow suit during the coming years to allow redevelopment of the area. No. 60007 *Sir Nigel Gresley* emerged from Doncaster Works in November 1937 and initially the locomotive had the maximum cut-off set at 65% with valve travel of 5¾in., as did the rest of the A4 Class. During World War Two, as a result of the heavy trains that were prevalent, the maximum cut-off was increased to 75% to help the locomotives when setting off and maximum valve travel was also increased to 6⅝in. An improvement was noticed and it was decided that this should be a class-wide modification. LNER no. 4499 *Sir Murrough Wilson* was the first to be changed, but there was no urgent progress and the last, BR no. 60005 *Sir Charles Newton*, was not altered until May 1957. *Sir Nigel Gresley* was also altered fairly late in May 1955.

GLASGOW ST ROLLOX SHED 45497

Visiting St Rollox from Perth is 'Black Five' no. 45497. The engine was allocated to the latter shed from at least September 1950 until October 1961; it had seen in Nationalisation at Motherwell shed. No. 45497 was built at Derby Works in April 1944 and was fitted with boiler no. 11328, which had 28 elements, dome regulator and separate top feed, two washout plugs on the first boiler ring and steel and copper firebox stays. In June 1958 the locomotive received a later boiler that differed slightly in carrying the revised top feed on the first boiler ring and this is illustrated here. Also, a LMS no. 5 snowplough is fitted to the bufferbeam and this was a common appendage for members of the class working in Scotland during the winter. The plough was positioned 4½in. above the rails and could be used when snowfall was reaching heights up to 2ft. BR introduced a new snowplough (designated no. 6 type) in 1950, which did not protrude from the front as much as the no. 5 plough and this could be also be found fitted to a number of former LMS classes. After leaving Perth, no. 45497 moved to Corkerhill, Ardrossan and Ayr, arriving at the latter in August 1962 to see out its career, which ended in February 1964.

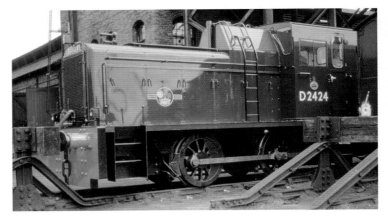

GLASGOW ST ROLLOX SHED D2424

BR Class 06 diesel-mechanical 0-4-0 locomotive D2424 was erected by Andrew Barclay, Sons & Co. Ltd in April 1959. Thirty five were produced by the company and they featured Gardner 8-cylinder 4-stroke engines, with Wilson-Drewry CA5 5-speed gearbox, Vulcan-Sinclair type C3 fluid coupling and Wiseman type 15 reversing gearbox and final drive. The locomotives were built for use in Scotland, but they had a short lifespan and only ten were in service to receive a TOPS number. D2424 left service in August 1972 and later scrapped: it has been photographed next to St Rollox shed's repair shop, which was located on the south side of the building. The shed was brought into use to replace Buchanan Street and St Rollox Works sheds, which were more than inadequate in their proportions for the requirements that were placed on them. Opened officially on 13 November 1916, the building was made from brick and had a transverse multi-pitched roof that covered 12 tracks.

GLASGOW YOKER SHED 57259

The two-track Yoker shed was opened by the CR during 1907 and was a sub-shed of Dawsholm. From the start of its operational life the former was home to smaller 0-6-0, 0-6-0T and 0-4-0ST engines and in the early days these were employed on the Rothesay Dock, transporting an array of goods around the city. In LMS and BR days locomotives could be sent to work in Scotstown or Robroyston goods yards. The facilities at the shed included a coal stage, water tank and second-hand 60ft. turntable. The locomotive featured at the shed is an early example of a CR Drummond 'Jumbo' goods engine that was built by Neilson & Co. during September 1884 as CR no. 525. Rebuilding of the engine was carried out in 1921 and after Grouping the locomotive received LMS no. 17259. The locomotive was a long-term resident at the shed under BR and was withdrawn in October 1962 after an impressive 78 year-long career. Diesel shunters had been present at Yoker since 1956 and were present for a time after steam had left the shed in January 1964. The buildings were eventually removed and Yoker Sports Centre now occupies the ground.

GLENEAGLES STATION 45473

Gleneagles Station was opened on 14 March 1856 as Crieff Junction and was located on the Scottish Central Railway line between the Caledonian Railway main line at Greenhill Upper Junction and Perth. The station also served as a terminus for the Crieff Junction Railway, which joined the SCR line with the town of Crieff and two railways present there - the Crieff & Comrie Railway and the Crieff & Methaven Junction Railway. The CJR was taken over by the SCR in June 1865 and the SCR was in turn amalgamated into the CR during the same year. In April 1912 the station was renamed Gleneagles and was later rebuilt by the CR in 1919. The Crieff branch was a casualty of the Beeching Report, despite efforts to improve receipts on the line with a Railbus service and it was closed on the 6 July 1964 with the track later being lifted. Stanier Class Five no. 45473 has been pictured after it has stopped at the Crieff branch line platform, which was subsequently removed, and is now the station's car park. The locomotive was made at Derby Works in May 1943 and was the second locomotive to be completed in order no. 3836, which had originally been placed at Crewe in July 1938, and delayed because of the war. The boiler used would have been the same as no. 45497 mentioned earlier, with no. 45473 being similarly fitted here with a later boiler. No. 45473 was withdrawn in November 1966.

GLENEAGLES STATION 60004

Leaving Gleneagles station with a Glasgow Buchanan Street-bound express is another locomotive from Aberdeen's A4 contingent - no. 60004 *William Whitelaw*. The engine had been manufactured at Doncaster Works and entered service as LNER no. 4462 *Great Snipe*. This name was a feature of the locomotive until it was replaced by *William Whitelaw* in July 1941. Another characteristic of the locomotive that was subsequently changed was the tender. At first tender no. 5667, of the streamlined non-corridor type, was attached and this was carried until July 1941. LNER no. 4482 (BR no. 60023) *Golden Eagle* then utilised it until withdrawn in October 1964. From July 1941 until February 1948 *William Whitelaw* had tender no. 5323, which was the first of the 1928 corridor tenders built for the non-stop services. This had previously been coupled with LNER no. 4472 *Flying Scotsman*, no. 4476 *Royal Lancer*, no. 4475 *Flying Fox* and no. 4482 *Golden Eagle*. It was later carried by BR no. 60022 *Mallard* and no. 60029 *Woodcock*. After losing tender no. 5323, no. 60004 carried streamlined non-corridor tender no. 5639, which had originally been allocated to A3 no. 2507 *Singapore*. The tender was then reserved for A4 no. 4903 *Peregrine* which took it into service from new until May 1939 when no. 4468 *Mallard* took possession. *William Whitelaw* had no. 5639 between February and May 1948 at which time the locomotive received the tender it is seen with here. No. 5484 was the corridor tender first carried by W1 Class 4-6-4 no. 10000 (BR no. 60700) and it was made to tender order no. 54 in 1929, featuring wheels with disc centres instead of spokes and the capacity was nine tons of coal and 5,000 gallons of water. No. 60004 carried this tender until withdrawn in July 1966. Tender no. 5484 was then taken by no. 60009 *Union of South Africa* to be preserved as its tender had been bought to carry water behind no. 4472 *Flying Scotsman*. Tender no. 5639 was used by no. 60700 until withdrawn in June 1959 apart from a few weeks in July 1953 when no. 60010 *Dominion of Canada* utilised it. The track for the Crieff branch line is visible in the immediate foreground of the picture.

HAMILTON SHED 57447

Stored at Hamilton shed, minus buffers, is a locomotive which was built for the CR. No. 57447 (CR no. 578) is a McIntosh-designed 'Jumbo' goods locomotive and it was erected at St Rollox Works during December 1896 as part of order Y47. The five locomotives made in this order were unique amongst the 'Jumbo' engines as they were built with condensing gear so they could operate on the Glasgow Central Railway line, which ran partly underground. An intercepting valve, operated by a series of rods and a crank, stopped used steam entering the blastpipe and diverted it into a pipe that diverged and left the smokebox. Two copper pipes then ran the length of the boiler at either sides transporting the steam into the cab where there was a connection to the tender. It is unknown when this apparatus was removed from the locomotives. No. 57447 worked a good proportion of its career from Polmadie shed and is carrying its shed code here. A transfer to Hamilton had been completed during September 1958 and the engine was in service until October 1962. The shed closed to steam the following month and was later used to house DMUs before it was demolished in the early 1980s. The building to the right is the shed's sand kiln and the ten track shed is out of view to the right.

HAMILTON SIDINGS 56256

Photographed at Hamilton shed shunting locomotive coal wagons at the coal stage, is no. 56256 - a former CR 782 Class 0-6-0T. It had been built by St Rollox Works in June 1898 and was operational until June 1959. The ramped coal stage with water tank as the roof had been installed with the shed in 1884. Hamilton shed was located on the north east side of Hamilton West station, which had been opened by the CR on 10 September 1849. The locomotive was noted at Hamilton during the 1930s, was there again at Nationalisation, and worked for BR from the shed. In the main, locomotives at Hamilton were employed on goods services particularly moving coal from the collieries in the area.

HAWICK SHED 78046

In Hawick shed's yard is a Standard Class 2 2-6-0, no. 78046, which was one of two initially allocated there. No. 78047 had also arrived with the locomotive and the main locations of their early duties were Riccarton Junction and Whitrope where the gradient necessitated the employment of a banking engine. Pick-up freight on the former Lauder Light Railway line was also a task given to the class, as was an occasional passenger service to Newcastle. By the early-1960s, two more Standard Class 2s had arrived at Hawick - nos. 78048 and 78049, both from St. Margaret's. Other duties found for the locomotives included local passenger services on and around the Waverley route. No. 78046 left for Bathgate in January 1964 and in September 1966 moved to St. Margaret's to see out its final days. The other members of the class gradually left Hawick and no. 78049 was present for the shed's closure in January 1966.

HAWICK STATION 60035

Hawick station was opened by the NBR 29 October 1849, but the station was then re-sited slightly to the south for the completion of the second phase of the Waverley line between Hawick and Carlisle. The station was on a curve with part of the two platforms extending onto the viaduct which allowed the line to cross the River Teviot. The station was built from stone and had two floors that accommodated waiting rooms, offices, booking office, toilet and stationmaster's quarters. Photographed heading a service to Carlisle is Gresley A3 Pacific no. 60035 *Windsor Lad*. The fitting of sine wave superheater elements to this locomotive and the nine other A3s in the final batch was quickly realised to have been a bad decision and they were subsequently removed from the locomotives to be replaced by standard elements. The sine wave elements had also been fitted to LNER Class P2 2-8-2 no. 2001 *Cock o' the North*, performing slightly better, but were subject to rapid wear. The elements were 1¼in. diameter, 11 swg and had a heating surface of 695 sq. ft., which was less than the standard elements. The station closed on 6 January 1969, but was not demolished until January 1975 and the viaduct was removed in the latter part of the year.

◆ HAWICK SHED 62483

Hawick shed was situated on the west side of Hawick station and the former had been opened by the NBR during the latter part of 1849. The shed contained two roads and was constructed using stone, making it durable enough for the shed to remain largely unaltered over the years; a leisure centre now occupies the land. No. 62483 *Glen Garry* was built by Cowlairs Works in March 1919. It is pictured in store at Hawick, where it was resident only 14 months between February 1958 to April 1959 when it was withdrawn, having come to the shed from St. Margaret's. When in steam the locomotive might have been found on a local passenger service as could four other 'Glens' allocated to the shed around this period.

HELENSBURGH CENTRAL STATION 67628

Helensburgh Central station was opened on 31 May 1858 by the Glasgow, Dumbarton & Helensburgh Railway and was the company's terminus for their line, which connected to the Edinburgh & Glasgow Railway at Cowlairs Junction. The E&GR subsequently took over the GD&HR in 1862. The station name did not include 'Central' until 8 June 1953. This V1 locomotive was built at Doncaster Works in December 1934 and it was the first member of the class to appear since 1931. Twenty-six were to be built as part of the 1930 building programme, but because of the depression there was a significant delay and the order was eventually cut to six. When completed these engines were allocated to Scotland and no. 67628, as LNER no. 2928, found itself at Parkhead shed to work local passenger services. Some Eastfield V1/V3s were put to work from Helensburgh shed working local services up to its closure in the early-1960s and they appear to be the only class of locomotive allocated there under BR. No. 67628 moved to Eastfield from Parkhead in November 1961 and spent a year there before leaving for Heaton in December 1962. A quick transfer to Gateshead followed and the locomotive spent its final years moving empty coaches and goods around the Newcastle area. Withdrawal came in November 1964.

INVERNESS SHED 61792

The engine was built by Kitson & Co. during August 1921 and given GNR no. 1702. The GNR H3 Class locomotives built by Kitson & Co. cost the former company £10,036 per engine, which when compared to the agreed price of £3,800 for the locomotives that were to be built by Beyer, Peacock & Co. in 1915, was a significant increase. This order was subsequently transferred to the NBLC and the original fee quoted by Beyer, Peacock & Co. was split proportionally between the two companies, as the latter had carried out some initial construction work. The locomotive was at first allocated to Peterborough New England shed, but by 1925 it was chosen for a move to Scotland. Before the switch could be completed modifications had to be made to some of the external features of the engine so it conformed with the NBR loading gauge. A 1ft. 2in. tall chimney replaced the 1ft. 7½in. chimney first fitted and the dome was flattened by 2¾in. Also, the roof was lowered by 3in. and the whistle was repositioned from the cab roof to behind the safety valves. The alterations were carried out by Doncaster Works between March and June 1925, but the engine reappeared there between 1-16 July for light work before returning to New England. The move north to Glasgow Eastfield was completed in August and LNER no. 4702 then moved to St. Margaret's during December, beginning a 17 year allocation at the shed. After leaving Doncaster Works the locomotive never returned and was subsequently maintained by Cowlairs Works as were all the K2s in Scotland. The engine was the only one repaired by Gateshead Works, this taking place between October and November 1931 after a coming together with a C7 4-4-2 at Blaydon. No. 61792 was also in the minority that went to Inverurie Works for light attention. In April 1934 Cowlairs altered the cab so it included side windows and extended the cab roof at the rear by 9in. The GNR class B tenders for the engines built by outside contractors were provided by the GNR and made at Doncaster. They had a capacity of 3,500 gallons of water and space for 6½ tons of coal. The tenders were later modified, beginning in 1940, to have two footsteps and a handrail on the left hand side only and this is visible here. Also on display here is a unique dome for a K2 as it is flat-topped, whereas the others were curved and this distinctive feature was carried from mid-1939 until no. 61792 was withdrawn from Keith shed in September 1960. Disposal was carried out by Inverurie Works.

INVERNESS SHED 57575

Illustrated here is a member of the CR McIntosh 812 Class of 0-6-0s, which was manufactured by Neilson, Reid & Co. in December 1899. The class had 5ft. diameter driving wheels, two inside cylinders, Stephenson motion and slide valves. In 1948 the locomotive was allocated to Corkerhill shed and was not moved on until September 1957. The locomotive arrived at Inverness at this time and was stationed at the shed until withdrawn in October 1959.

◆ INVERNESS SHED 45475

A conference between the engine's crew and shed staff appears to have been in progress allowing Stanier 'Black Five' no. 45475 to pose for the camera. The locomotive was the first of two members of the class to be constructed at Derby Works in June 1943. Attached at this time was tender no. 9819, which was of the Mark 2 welded variety. The frames of the tender were 1in. thick with additional support provided by longitudinal frames ½in. deep. Six 4ft. 3in. diameter wheels with triangular-section rims were used, with the wheelbase being 7ft. 6in and 7ft. 6in. The total length of the tender was approx. 24ft. 2½in long and 21ft. of this was devoted to the water tank. The rear, side and floor plates were ¼in. steel. The total weight of the Mark Two tender was 26 tons 16 cwt, which was 1 ton 2 cwt lighter than the Mark One riveted tender. No. 45475 used this latter type between November 1956 and March 1957, replacing a Mark One part welded tender that had been in use previously. In this picture the tender is a Mark Two example, but it would again be replaced by the Mark One riveted version during the 1960s. A boiler with top feed on the first ring would also be fitted from mid-1963 to the locomotive's withdrawal in September 1966. No. 45475 was allocated to Perth shed from possibly 1944 until it left service.

INVERNESS SHED 54493

The first shed at Inverness was opened by the Inverness & Nairn Railway on 5 November 1855 at the same time as Inverness station, which was also opened by the company. It was on the north side of the line to Nairn and east of the station. The shed was only a small structure but was subsequently extended before it closed in September 1863. A new facility was built by the Inverness & Aberdeen Junction Railway at this time and it was located to the south of the Nairn line, further to the east of the station. The new building was larger than the earlier structure and was a semi-roundhouse. However, this was considerably extended by the Highland Railway in 1875 as they added five roads to each end of the building. The original turntable was 45ft., the size later increasing to 55ft. Pictured on the shed's turntable is an example of Pickersgill's 72 Class of 4-4-0s. It was built by Armstrong Whitworth & Co. Ltd in May 1921 as CR no. 88. The locomotive was at Aviemore shed from at least Nationalisation until July 1954 when relocated to Inverness. The locomotive ceased its duties in November 1961. The shed was modified by BR in the late-1940s with the removal of the stone archways over the tracks and steel beams were utilised instead for clearance reasons. Closure came in mid-1961 and the site was cleared in 1963. A supermarket and car park now occupy the area.

INVERURIE 40606

The Fowler upgrade of the Midland Railway design of 4-4-0 eradicated some of the flaws associated with the latter locomotives. The inside cylinders were a noted problem on the MR engines and it was originally envisaged that the new ones would have outside cylinders, however, restrictions on the intended routes precluded this idea from further development. The inside cylinders were redesigned instead with the boiler pressure increased and the driving wheel diameter reduced to further improve the MR 4-4-0 design. This member of the class was erected at Derby Works in November 1928. The locomotive was a long-term resident at Ardrossan shed, apart from a sojourn at Carstairs shed between October and November 1958. No. 40606 was condemned in May 1959. The locomotive could be at Inverurie Works to be scrapped as could its classmate, no. 40610, stood to the right.

INVERURIE WORKS 64572

This J37 0-6-0 looks resplendent after visiting Inverurie Works paint shop. The paint shop measured 242ft. by 122ft. and was located on the west side of the north end of site adjacent to the carriage and wagon shop. The locomotive had been built by the NBLC's Atlas Works in August 1918. As LNER no. 9314 the engine was fitted with Raven cab signalling sometime between 1927 and 1928, but it, as well as others similarly fitted, only carried the apparatus for a relatively short time as it was removed on all between 1934 and 1935. No. 64572 was later fitted with AWS and the protection plate is visible here. The locomotive was allocated to St. Margaret's shed until withdrawal in September 1964.

INVERURIE WORKS 57612

A need for new works arose out of the inadequacies in size of the Great North of Scotland Railway's works at Kittybrewster. In 1892 investigations into a new site and layout had been begun by the company, but construction on the 24 acre site did not begin until 1898. As well as the works approx. 118 houses were built by the GNSR for employees on the land and recreation facilities were also provided for them. The works consisted of; boiler shop, erecting shop, fitting shop, power house (all of these in one building measuring 290ft. by 270ft.), smithy, stores, carriage and wagon shops, offices and paint shop. Only a number of 4-4-0s were built at the works before its role became the maintenance of locomotives. The site was utilised by the LNER and then BR until closure in December 1969. This freshly painted CR 812 Class 0-6-0 was constructed by Dübs & Co. during May 1900. The locomotive has made the long trip from Dawsholm for this picture; it was allocated there until September 1959. No. 57612 had completed its time in service in April 1962 and was sent to be scrapped from Grangemouth shed.

KEITH SHED 61783

No. 61783, a LNER K2, was completed by Kitson & Co. in July 1921; one of nine produced during the month. In March 1933 the locomotive acquired the name *Loch Sheil* as it was a regular on the West Highland line from Glasgow Eastfield shed. Twelve other K2s were named between February 1933 (LNER no. 4692 *Loch Eil*) and June 1934 (LNER no. 4699 *Loch Laidon*). Only one was from outside the Kitson & Co. batch of locomotives; LNER no. 4674 *Loch Arkaig*, which was erected by the NBLC's Queens Park Works in July 1918. The nameplate of *Loch Sheil* carried the incorrect spelling of the Loch near the West Highland line between Fort William and Mallaig at Glenfinnan as it should be Loch Shiel. This mistake was carried by the locomotive from naming until withdrawal. No. 61783 switched bases from Eastfield to Fort William in October 1939 and was resident there until April 1953 when it returned to Eastfield. This was a brief residency as it had returned north by July. In June 1954 a move to Aberdeen Kittybrewster shed on the east coast occurred, but by September 1956 *Loch Sheil* was stationed at Keith where it could be utilised on local passenger and goods services as well as empty coach movements. No. 61783 left service in June 1959 and was later scrapped by T.W. Ward, Wishaw.

KEITH SIDINGS 54472

No. 54472 was made by the NBLC in May 1916 and initially carried CR no. 933. At Nationalisation it was allocated to Inverness and was resident there until March 1953. It then moved to Forres, working from the shed until June 1959 and was presumably resident here when the picture was taken as the next move was south to Corkerhill. The locomotive appears to have been unwanted at the shed as it was moved to St Rollox and then Polmadie during July and it was withdrawn from the latter shed in October 1959.

KEITH SIDINGS 65277

Heading a coal train at Keith is a LNER J36 Class 0-6-0. The locomotive had been built for the NBR at Cowlairs Works in June 1896 and was part of their C Class, which were designed by M. Holmes. The design emulated the Drummond   0-6-0s and featured a few modifications that included an increased number of tubes and a level grate. The class were built between 1888 and 1900, with a total of 168 locomotives being produced. In 1913 the NBR began the process of rebuilding the engines and this task lasted until after Grouping into 1923. This locomotive was rebuilt in June 1922 and the main alterations were the fitting of a new larger boiler and a cab with side windows. The boiler was 4ft. 8⅛in.; originally it had been 4ft. 6¼in. diameter. The total heating surface of the larger boiler was 1214 sq. ft. and the boiler pressure was 160psi; this was later increased by 5psi from 1926. No. 65277 was allocated to Bathgate shed during the 1950s but by September 1959 it was working from Keith shed. This lasted until April 1961 and the locomotive returned to Bathgate, which is where it was withdrawn from in June 1963.

KEITH SHED 40648

No. 40648 was constructed at Crewe Works during September 1931 with 19in. by 26in. cylinders, boiler pressure of 180psi and 6ft. 9in. diameter driving wheels. For comparison the MR 483 Class, which the LMS 2Ps were based on, had 20½in. by 26in. cylinders, 160psi boiler pressure and 7ft. 0½in. driving wheels when rebuilt by Fowler. The locomotive was allocated to Ayr at Nationalisation, moving in April 1954 to Aberdeen Kittybrewster shed. No. 40648 has probably worked a local passenger service to Keith from Aberdeen here in the picture. The engine was briefly moved to Aberdeen Ferryhill in August 1961 but was condemned a month later in September.

◆ KEITH SHED 54472

The section of the Inverness & Aberdeen Junction Railway between Elgin and Keith was the final part of the line to be opened on 18 August 1858. The company's locomotive shed was also opened on this date and the building had four roads covered by a twin gable roof. It was located to the west of the station and was on the north side of the line, but it was later downsized to two roads and the materials were reutilized at Blair Atholl shed. The Great North of Scotland Railway had opened a shed two years previously in October 1856 and this also had four tracks, enclosed by a stone structure. This was located on the opposite side of the station and on the south side of the line. The 1858 shed was closed at Nationalisation but the GNSR shed was active until January 1961. It serves as a backdrop for CR Pickersgill 4-4-0 no. 54472 and visible are the 1953 alterations, which saw the stone arches over the roads replaced by steel lintels and brick gables. The shed was used by diesel locomotives until the mid-1970s.

KELSO SIDINGS 65233

Bill has captured this interesting picture of J36 no. 65233 derailed at Kelso Sidings. The locomotive was built by Cowlairs Works during July 1891 and had been rebuilt by November 1913. During the First World War the engine was one of twenty five of the class to be used by the ROD in France on supply train duties. The locomotives were shipped to the continent between October and November 1917 and later returned to the NBR between April and July 1919. In recognition of their service the locomotives were given names related to the conflict. This locomotive, as NBR no. 657, received the name *Plumer* after General Sir Herbert Plumer, who was Commander of the British Second Army between 1915 and 1917. In some instances the name was removed during a visit to works and then reapplied at a later time. The engine first lost the name in May 1944, but it had been reapplied by December 1945. The end of the following year saw it removed again and it was not restored until August 1948 while at Cowlairs Works. Inverurie Works had stripped the name from the locomotive on the previous occasions and they deleted it again in January 1956 and it did not reappear. *Plumer* was allocated to Polmont shed in January 1948 and it was December 1958 before the engine saw its first transfer under BR to Hawick. The following December no. 65233 had moved to Bathgate and was sent for scrap during December 1960.

KELSO STATION 78046

Kelso was the meeting place for the North Eastern Railway's Kelso Branch from the east coast main line and the NBR's Kelso line from the Waverley route. The NBR line originally terminated at Wallace Nick, with a temporary terminus operating from 17 June 1850 until Kelso station was opened on 27 January 1851. The station house contained the booking office and waiting rooms on the ground floor, with the Stationmaster's rooms on the second floor. The NBR section of the line originally had two tracks but this was reduced to one between Kelso Junction and Roxburgh from November 1933. No. 78046 was built at Darlington Works in October 1955 as part of a batch of ten destined for the Scottish Region. All 65 Standard Class 2 2-6-0s were completed at Darlington between December 1952 and November 1956. The locomotive is seen at the south platform with a passenger service from Berwick-upon-Tweed and would proceed to St Boswells. The Kelso line closed to passenger traffic on 15 June 1964, but goods services continued until 1 April 1968. No. 78046 was removed from its duties in November 1966 and was scrapped by Arnott Young, Old Kilpatrick, during the following year.

KILLIN JUNCTION STATION 55260

A LMS-built example of the CR 439 Class design is seen with a passenger service at Killin Junction station. No. 55260 was the first of these locomotives to be constructed by Nasmyth Wilson in May 1925. Between 1948 and May 1952 the engine was allocated to Hurlford shed then moving to Beattock. The remainder of the decade was spent at the shed before a transfer to Perth in December 1960, followed by a move to Oban in February 1961. No. 55260 returned to Perth in June 1962 and was withdrawn at the end of the year. Killin Junction station was opened by the Callander & Oban Railway on 1 April 1886 for the transfer of passengers to the Killin Railway. Passengers who wanted to travel to other destinations along the railway line using the station were not permitted to do so until pressure was applied to the company by locals and it soon relented. The station closed on 28 September 1965.

KILLIN STATION 57339

Killin station was also opened on 1 April 1886, but by the Killin Railway, which ran between Killin Junction, Killin and Loch Tay. A station called Killin had previously been opened on the Callander and Oban Railway line on 1 June 1870 but this was renamed Glenoglehead Crossing. Services between Killin and Loch Tay stations were stopped in April 1921 because of a coal strike and they later resumed only in the summer months. This persisted until 9 September 1939 when Loch Tay station was closed permanently, however, the locomotive shed remained in use until the line was closed as a result of the landslip at Glen Ogle in September 1965. This Smellie 'Jumbo' 0-6-0, no. 57339, is pictured awaiting departure with the Killin to Killin Junction service.

KILMARNOCK STATION 40651

This Fowler 4-4-0 is stood at the present platform two at Kilmarnock station with the 16.09 service to Ardrossan. The locomotive was built at Crewe Works in September 1931. It was at Corkerhill shed in 1948 and moved from there to Motherwell in October 1952 and thus earning the distinction of being the only member of the class to reside there for BR. No. 40651 was at Corkerhill again in May 1953 but moved south to Carlisle Kingmoor in October 1954 for a five year-long allocation. The engine briefly joined the Hurlford contingent of the class from August to November 1959, returning to Carlisle at this latter date. A final return to Corkerhill occurred in February 1960 before the locomotive saw out its career at Hurlford. The final month in operation for no. 40651 was November 1961.

KILMARNOCK STATION 77015

BR Standard Class 3 2-6-0 no. 77015 was erected at Swindon Works during July 1954 and it travelled via the east coast main line to its first allocation at Hurlford shed. This was the only allocation for the locomotive and the same can be said for three of the other four Standard Class 3s at the shed. From Hurlford, located on the outskirts of Kilmarnock, the class could be used at this latter place as the station pilot or services from there to destinations such as the Ayrshire coast and Glasgow. They also had a role on branch passenger services between Ayr and Dalmellington and Muirkirk and Lanark. Local services between Ayr and Ardrossan were also transferred to the class from LMS 4-4-0s. In

addition, colliery trips were not an uncommon duty for the engines. However, much of the branch work had been eliminated by 1964/1965 and withdrawals of the class from Hurlford began in March 1966. No. 77015 followed in July and the remainder were condemned in November. The locomotive had been sent to G.H. Campbell, Airdrie, for scrapping by the end of the year.

KILMARNOCK STATION 45009

At Grouping the LMS inherited 393 classes that lacked standardisation and a robust mixed traffic engine. The appointment of W.A. Stanier in early-1932 gave the LMS the opportunity to remedy some of the shortcomings of their motive power, which had not been adequately addressed up to this point. The LNWR 'Prince of Wales' Class 4-6-0s were also getting ready for major overhaul at this time, having already showed up failings in their design and components, so the opportunity was taken for a new mixed traffic 4-6-0 to be designed to replace this class and a number of other pre-Grouping classes. The new design was to have a wide route availability and standardisation of parts for ease of maintenance and repair. Stanier brought some GWR features to the boiler design with the use of a taper boiler and low-degree of superheat. The new locomotives were ordered from the Vulcan Foundry, who were to manufacture 50 as part of the 1934 building programme. This order was followed up by an order for twenty placed at Crewe Works in the 1935 building programme; this locomotive, as LMS no. 5009, left the works in March 1935. After experience gained from the first of the Vulcan Foundry engines in service it was realised that the low-degree of superheat was inadequate for the satisfactory operation of the engines, as had similarly been seen with the Jubilees and the Princess Royal Classes. As a result the boiler was redesigned to include a 21 element superheater (increased from 14 elements used previously), which had 5⅛in. diameter flues, 1⅛in. diameter elements 11 swg thick and had a total heating surface of 256 sq. ft. Also, the firebox had a vertical throatplate, the regulator was mounted on the side smokebox and the top feed had a dome-like cover. As no. 5009, the locomotive was initially fitted with boiler no. 8826 of the 21 element variety. The engine was at Carlisle Kingmoor for Nationalisation but by the start of the 1950s had reached Motherwell and it spent the rest of its career based from the shed. No. 45009 was condemned in November 1965.

KILMARNOCK STATION 45124

The 50 locomotives in the second order placed at Vulcan Foundry replaced an order for 30 Jubilee Class engines in the 1935 building programme and a further five Class 5s were commissioned from Crewe. The estimated cost of the Vulcan Foundry engines, given in *LMS Locomotive Profiles No. 5* (2003), was £5,540 each. As LMS no. 5124, the locomotive was the last of the second batch from Vulcan Foundry to be constructed and it entered traffic in July 1935 fitted with a 21 element boiler, no. 9054. Subsequently a domed 24 element boiler was carried between June 1938 and July 1942 and a sloping throatplate boiler was fitted between January 1951 and June 1955. Fitting of this latter type necessitated modifying the frames by bringing forward the frame stay in front of the throatplate and altering the dragbox. In this picture no. 45124 has reverted to the 21 element type boiler, but has acquired a transverse top feed cover instead of the type usually fitted to this type of boiler. The engine is also seen fitted with AWS and tablet exchange apparatus. For the second half of the 1930s the locomotive worked from Edge Hill shed but by 1944 the allocation had changed to Inverness. No. 45124 appears to have stayed at Inverness until May 1960 when it moved to Corkerhill. Hurlford was reached in January 1961 and was active from here for a considerable period before moves to Corkerhill, Motherwell and Polmadie rounded off its career. The end came in May 1967.

KILMARNOCK STATION 40602

This Fowler 4-4-0 is pictured at Kilmarnock station, at the present platform one, with the 16.13 Kilmarnock to Ayr branch passenger service. Kilmarnock has had a long association with railways as a horse-drawn system operated by the Kilmarnock & Troon Railway was in use from 6 July 1812 for goods and 1818 for passengers. The system was later upgraded to use a steam locomotive. The Glasgow, Paisley Kilmarnock & Ayr Railway then proposed to build a line in 1836 between these places and after receiving Royal Assent in 1837 construction began with the first section opening in 1839. Kilmarnock station was subsequently opened on 4 April 1843. No. 40602 was constructed in November 1928 at Derby Works. It was a Hurlford engine at this time and was one of 41 members of the class to be resident there under BR. The locomotive had a number of spells at Carlisle Kingmoor and Corkerhill as well during the BR period and it left service in October 1961 from Hurlford.

KILMARNOCK STATION 40661

A Fowler 4-4-0 is heading out of the east side of Kilmarnock station and over the 23-arch viaduct, with the Kilmarnock to Darvel branch passenger service. This branch left the former Glasgow, Paisley, Kilmarnock & Ayr Railway line at Hurlford Junction and was built in sections from the 1840s. Darvel station was opened on 1 June 1896 by the Glasgow & South Western Railway and the line was later extended by the company and the CR to Strathaven. However, this extension closed on 11 September 1939 and services on the Darvel branch terminated on 6 April 1964. No. 40661 entered traffic from Derby Works during December 1931 and was in service until November 1961. The engine was employed by BR from Hurlford shed. Seen behind the tender is the former West High Church of Scotland, which was built in 1844 and is now business premises, while behind the locomotive is another church, High Church, built in the 1730s.

KILMARNOCK STATION 77015

Only 20 Standard Class 3 2-6-0s were ever constructed and these were initially split evenly between the North Eastern Region (Darlington) and Scottish Region (Dawsholm, Hamilton, Blair Atholl and Hurlford). All of the class were built at Swindon Works and they entered traffic between February and September 1954. A further five members of the class were ordered, but after change of requirements, the order was put on hold and was eventually cancelled in 1956. Swindon was responsible for the design, with some features being contributed by the drawing offices at Doncaster, Derby and Brighton. The boiler was based on the GWR no. 2 boiler fitted to a number of the company's tank engines. The BR6 boiler fitted to the Standard Class 3s was 5ft. 0½in. diameter tapering to 4ft. 5in. and 10ft. 10½in. in length between the tubeplates. There were 143 small tubes of 1⅝in. diameter that gave a heating surface of 924 sq. ft. An 18 element superheater was employed with 5⅛in. diameter flues and 1⅜in. diameter elements, which gave a heating surface of 184 sq. ft. The firebox was 7ft. long by 4ft. wide and the grate area was 20.38 sq. ft. The boiler worked at 200psi. Two cylinders were also used and these were 17½in. diameter by 28in. stroke with 10in. piston valves and Walschaerts valve gear. All members of the class received a BR2A tender when built. No. 77015 is photographed at the head of the 17.46 Kilmarnock to Lugton branch passenger service.

KILMARNOCK STATION 57295 ✦

The order for Drummond's penultimate batch of 0-6-0 goods locomotives was placed in October 1886 and 12 were constructed to order no. Y12 at St Rollox Works between May and August 1887. This locomotive left the works in June 1887. The engines in order no. Y12 featured a revised exhaust passage from the cylinders to the blastpipe, which was also of a new pattern. The vortex blastpipe, designed by William Adams, was fitted to the Y12 engines as well as Smellie's only order for 0-6-0s. During the first years of the 1900s however, the use of vortex blastpipe was discontinued on the locomotives fitted and they received a normal blastpipe in its place at an unknown time. As CR no. 340, the engine would have originally carried the CR blue livery, but at Grouping the LMS changed this to unlined black with 'LMS' on the cab side and the engine's LMS number on the side of the tender. The letters were gold blocked with black and backed by vermilion, while the number was 18in. high in gold transfers. A problem arose in the placing of this information when tenders needed repairs or maintenance, they could not be switched between engines without a costly renumbering. It was decided in 1928 to switch the number to the cab and the company's initials to the tender. The number and 'LMS' were 12in. and 14in. high respectively and both were applied in gold transfers. No. 57295 is seen here with a stovepipe chimney, which was an alteration applied to the class by the LMS from the mid-1940s and the engine carried one from the end of 1944. Withdrawal came in June 1962 when no. 57295 was allocated to Hurlford shed.

♦ KINGUSSIE STATION 44704

A Perth-allocated 'Black Five' passes through Kingussie station with 10.00 Glasgow Buchanan Street to Inverness express passenger service. Kingussie station was opened by the Inverness & Perth Junction Railway on 9 September 1863 and it lies approx. 134 miles from Glasgow, 77½ miles from Perth, with another 40½ miles having to be negotiated before Inverness was reached. Approximately 18 miles from Kingussie, the ascent to Slochd Summit would begin and the line would rise at gradients of 1 in 60, 1 in 92 and 1 in 70 until the peak, 1,315 feet above sea level, was surmounted. The highest point on the rail network, Druimuachdar Pass 1,484 feet above sea level, had been passed earlier in the journey from Perth. No. 44704 had been built in September 1948 at Horwich Works. One hundred and twenty members of the class were erected there over a five year period, beginning in 1945. This was also the year that self-cleaning smokeboxes began to be fitted to the class. They were first seen on locomotives originated in America and in Britain because of the war. The aim of the arrangement was to eject detritus that had accumulated in the smokebox during the operation of the engine. It worked by deflecting flue gases, using baffle plates, under a plate where material had been deposited and the gas transported it through a wire screen to break it up or trap larger particles of waste. The smaller particles were then ejected into the atmosphere with the exhaust steam. The device also stopped wear to the tubes and they thus required less maintenance and lasted longer. No. 44704 has sans-serif typeface numbers on the smokebox numberplate, while the bufferbeam has previously been fitted with a snowplough. The locomotive left service in September 1966.

KIPPS SHED

KIPPS SHED 68114

LNER Y9 Class 0-4-0ST locomotive no. 68114 was made at Cowlairs in November 1897. It has been pictured by Bill at Kipps shed while undergoing maintenance as the connecting rod is missing from the engine – the culprits could be the characters to the left. No. 68114 could have been found working at Dundee Tay Bridge shed from 1948 to April 1958, apart from a month from March 1951 when it was on loan to RAF Leuchars. In April 1959 Kipps became the final residence for no. 68114 and removal from service occurred in September 1960.

KIPPS SHED 65285

NBR Class C, LNER Class J36, 0-6-0 no. 65285 was built at Cowlairs Works in November 1896; a total of four members of the class emerged from there during the month. The locomotive carried steam brakes throughout its time in service for the LNER and NBR, but pre-Grouping the engine was fitted with steam and vacuum brakes for an unknown length of time. As NBR no. 714, the locomotive was rebuilt by the company at the cusp of Grouping in November 1922. The vast majority of the class were attached to Holmes 2,500 gallon tenders which also had a coal capacity of six tons. February 1937 saw the engine slightly modified by the LNER to have a diminutive chimney and dome; two months later LNER no. 9716 (BR no. 65287) was also changed in this way as the locomotives were working on the Gartverrie branch, which had a low bridge that would have been fouled by the original fittings. Both engines remained in this state until withdrawn during November and June 1963 respectively. Nos. 65285 and 65287 had long-term allocations to Kipps shed, but they ended their careers at Dawsholm and Grangemouth.

KIPPS SHED 68443

A dropped fire smoulders in front of this J83 0-6-0T, which resided at Kipps throughout the BR period until the company condemned the locomotive in February 1961. The first shed at Kipps was constructed on the eastern approach to Coatbridge Sunnyside station during 1837. The Monkland & Kirkintilloch Railway were responsible and they had been operating in the area for just over ten years, predominantly moving mineral traffic around the area. The line was taken over by the Edinburgh & Glasgow Railway then the NBR. The latter company used a new shed from 1890 (to the west of the first destroyed in a fire during the same year), which had previously been used in the erection of the Forth Bridge, and it contained three tracks. It was in use until January 1963 when BR switched the focus of the facilities to diesel traction. This function was discontinued in the latter half of the 1960s and the site has since been cleared and now partly used for commercial premises. No. 68443 had been the second member of the class to be constructed in August 1900 by Neilson, Reid & Co. It was rebuilt by the LNER in June 1924.

KYLE OF LOCHALSH STATION 44978

In the early-1860s a quicker land-based route from the north west of Scotland to the south was being sought. The Highland Railway became the driving force behind this venture and the Dingwall & Skye Railway was authorised on 5 July 1865. The 63 mile-long line was planned to run from the former Inverness & Ross-shire Railway line at Dingwall to Kyle of Lochalsh. However, the line was soon in trouble due to the vociferous objections from Sir William MacKenzie. This impasse was not surmounted until 1868 when the route of the line was modified to run further north, avoiding his home at Strathpeffer. The line from Strome Ferry to Kyle of Lochalsh was also omitted due to projected work and costs. The line was opened fully from 19 August 1870. Strome Ferry, on Loch Carron, proved to be an unsuitable place for a port and the continuation of the line to Kyle of Lochalsh, where the conditions were more favourable, was initiated. The Act was obtained on the 29 June 1893 and the extension was opened to traffic on 2 November 1897. No. 44978 was built at Crewe Works during June 1946. At Nationalisation BR assessed four different liveries, with three coming from constituent companies and the other originating from a pre-Grouping company. The London and North Western Railway black livery with red, grey and cream highlights was eventually chosen and began to be applied to the Class Fives from late-1948 to mid-1949. The locomotive was withdrawn from Perth in July 1965.

KYLE OF LOCHALSH D5322

At the present day platform one, on 14 June 1962 with the 17.30 service to Inverness, is a BR Class 26 diesel-electric locomotive, no. D5322, which was constructed by the Birmingham Railway Carriage & Wagon Co. Ltd in April 1959. As no. 26022, the locomotive was withdrawn in February 1981 and subsequently scrapped.

KYLE OF LOCHALSH STATION D5325

At platform two is D5322's classmate D5325, which was constructed by the BRCW in May 1959. Twenty had been initially ordered to Type 2 specifications as part of the Pilot Scheme and were followed by a further 27. BRCW was not a noted locomotive producer (but it was producing DMUs at the time), so it went into partnership with a number of other companies such as; Sulzer, Crompton Parkinson and Allen West to produce the components. The engines were initially scheduled to work from the London area and into the Southern Region, however, the SR Civil Engineer rejected them and a new role had to be found for them. This was found in Scotland, initially at Edinburgh and eventually extending to Inverness. D5325 was initially based at Edinburgh Haymarket before transferring to Inverness during July 1960 and from here the locomotive could be used on any of the Highland lines. Visible behind the locomotive is one of the 'Devon Belle' observation cars that was used on the Kyle of Lochalsh line from the 1960s. After being withdrawn in October 1993, D5325 was bought by the Highland Railway Diesel Locomotive Co. Ltd to become part of the Strathspey Railway collection. Twelve other Class 26s are preserved around the country.

LANARK STATION 45483

Lanark was joined to the CR main line by a branch line at Silvermuir Junction during the early-1850s and the station was opened on the 5 June 1855. The Douglas branch was then added to the line by the CR, opening on 1 April 1864, followed by a branch to Muirkirk, which opened in 1874 providing a connection with the G&SWR. The Douglas branch and the Muirkirk braches were closed on the 5 October 1964, but freight survived on the line between Ponfeigh and Lanark until 15 January 1968. Pictured with the 16.40 Lanark to Edinburgh Princes Street station is Stanier Class Five no. 45483. The locomotive was manufactured by Derby Works in September 1943, with boiler no. 11042 that had 28 Superheater Co. elements and a Mark Two welded tender, no. 9829. At one point the engine carried a Mark One riveted tender and later in its life the locomotive was noted with a boiler that had the top feed on the first boiler ring. The Class Five's had 6ft. diameter coupled wheels with 19 spokes and 3in. thick tyres secured by Gibson rings; axles were 8½in. diameter. Wheels fitted to the engines were initially balanced for 66⅔% of the reciprocating masses, but after the late-1930s this was changed to 50%. Experiments had been carried out by the LMS's Research Department prior to this decision being taken, using engines with the original setting, 50% and 30% balancing to look at how the setting affected wheel lifting and hammer blow to the track. A side-control bogie with lateral coil springs was fitted to the class and initially sideplay was set at 2¼in., but from LMS no. 5472 this was increased to 2¾in. The bogie wheels were 3ft. 3in. diameter with ten spokes and the wheelbase was 6ft. 6in. In 1948 no. 45483 was allocated to Motherwell shed, however, by the start of the 1950s the engine was sent to Perth and this stay lasted until October 1961. Dalry Road shed became the engine's new home until it was transferred to St. Margaret's shed in October 1965. Withdrawal occurred in December 1966. St Leonard's church seen in the background has since been demolished and replaced by a building that currently houses a job centre.

MALLAIG STATION 62052

The stone building to the left of the locomotive is Mallaig shed, which was located on the west side of Mallaig station. Entry was gained from the south end and the structure covered one track. The shed came in to operation on 1 April 1901 under the control of the West Highland Railway, later the NBR and LNER after Grouping. Mallaig shed was a sub-shed of Fort William and the shed codes under BR were 63D, 65J (May 1955) and 63B (June 1960) - placing this picture after this date. Mallaig closed to traffic on 18 June 1962 and the building survived until the late-1980s when it was demolished and the site is now occupied by the A830 road. Locomotive no. 62052 belonged to the K1 Class of 2-6-0s that were designed by A.H. Peppercorn, with the order being placed at the end of October 1947. The design had initially been prepared by Edward Thompson after he had rebuilt a member of the Gresley K4 Class. Peppercorn made only a few amendments to the design including making a gap in the running plate in front of the cylinders, reducing the size of the axle journals and helical springs were used instead of laminated springs in the pony truck. A total of 70 locomotives were constructed by the NBLC between May 1949 and March 1950. No. 62052 was built by the company at their Queens Park Works during November 1949.

MALLAIG STATION 62052

Fort William, the West Highland Railway's original terminus, was 40 miles by land and 100 miles by sea from the north western fishing territories. This traffic, it was hoped, would provide a lucrative alternative to the seasonal and unguaranteed passenger receipts that the line was relying on at the time. The connection was proposed to run between Banavie and Mallaig Bay, covering a distance of just over 39 miles. The Act for the railway was passed on 31 July 1894, however, construction could not go ahead without a proposed Government guarantee to the shareholder's dividend. This was not forthcoming, but after a short passage of time and a change in the political climate, the guarantee was agreed in 1896. The first sod of the extension was cut by Lady Margaret Cameron of Locheil on 21 January 1897. The Glasgow firms of Simpson & Wilson and Robert McAlpine & Sons were employed as the engineers and builders respectively. When completed the line featured eleven tunnels, 100 cuttings and a number of bridges. The first train left Mallaig on 1 April 1901 bound for Glasgow with the 7.20 passenger service. The station at Mallaig was unusual to the other stations, on both the old and new line, in that it had an island platform and locomotive no. 62052 is seen here at the present day platform 1 with the express service to Fort William. No. 62052 had been allocated to Fort William since May 1954 and the engine was withdrawn from there during December 1962 and later scrapped at Cowlairs. The fish traffic, that was hoped to bring riches to the line, was never substantial and for a number of years the line was making a loss for the WHR and later the NBR.

MALLAIG STATION 76001

Also near the shed is this Standard Class 4 2-6-0 and the shed's water tank can be seen to the right. No. 76001 was built at Horwich Works in December 1952. As with 76002 mentioned earlier, the locomotive was fitted with a BR7 boiler that was fabricated at Darlington. The firebox had an outside length of 7ft. 6in. and a width of 4ft. 0½in. The wrapper plate was ⅜in. wide, while the tubeplate was 1in. deep. The first of the locomotive's allocations was to Motherwell depot, but from April 1955 no. 76001 had a month's sojourn at Blair Atholl and was employed as a banking engine at Druimuachdar Summit, a task that was subsequently deemed unsuitable. In May and June 1960 transfers to Oban and Fort William occurred and from the latter the locomotive usually worked the 15.15 to Mallaig, returning to Fort William with the 17.40 passenger service. The engine had spells at Corkerhill and Ardrossan before its final allocation to Ayr and no. 76001 left service from there in August 1966.

MOTHERWELL SHED 90754

Long-term Motherwell resident no. 90754, stands in the shed's yard. This War Department 2-10-0 was built at the NBLC's Hyde Park Works in June 1945 as part of the second order for the class to be constructed and consisted of 50 engines. The first batch of 100 locomotives had been completed at the company's works between 1943 and 1944. Twenty of this first batch were sent to the Middle East, while the majority of the others remained in Britain working for the LMS and LNER until needed by the WD. No. 90754, WD no. 93778, never went to work in Europe as it was surplus to the WD's requirements by the time it was completed, so the LNER took it on loan from them between June 1945 and October 1946. The company based the locomotive at March shed and from there it worked on goods services. After returning to WD possession the locomotive was stored at Longmoor and had an uncertain future. After Nationalisation the remaining 25 WD 2-10-0s in Britain were bought for BR and they were then taken out of storage and earmarked for work in the Scottish Region. No. 90754 was overhauled at Ashford Works before beginning its BR career at Motherwell shed. The locomotive's career ended in June 1961 and the last of the class left service during 1962. Motherwell shed had been opened in March 1866 to serve the mineral requirements in the area. It was located to the north of Motherwell station and contained eight tracks, with a two road repair shop on the east side. A ramped coal stage could be found at both ends of the depot and by 1906 a 70ft. turntable was extant in the southern part of the site. The shed was virtually unchanged when closed by BR on 1 July 1967. The building was then transformed into a diesel shed and it retained this function until 2007.

NEWTON-ON-AYR STATION 42740

Pictured at Newton-on-Ayr station, perhaps with a coal train, is LMS Hughes 'Crab' 2-6-0 locomotive no. 42740, which was constructed at Crewe Works during March 1927. One hundred engines to the design were authorised during July 1924 but construction did not begin until late-1925 or early-1926. The work was split between Horwich and Crewe with the works completing 30 and 70 locomotives respectively. Those built at Crewe cost £5,712, while the engines from Horwich had a price tag of £6,070 each. The tender costs were almost the same; those from Horwich cost £1,067 and the Crewe examples cost £1,052. The difference was in the price of the engines, which were £5,003 from Horwich and £4,660 from Crewe. Further batches were constructed up to 1932, with the expenditure on each engine reducing slightly over this period. The locomotives in the final batch of ten that were built at Crewe cost a total of £4,979 to erect. The cab was in the Lancashire & Yorkshire Railway tradition and featured a centrally mounted regulator which was only fitted to the first 100. Later locomotives featured the LMS pull-up regulator and the earlier engines were afterwards changed to this type. The class were originally meant to have a new design of tender, but Hughes retired before construction began allowing incoming CME Sir Henry Fowler to substitute the new design for a Midland Railway 3,500 gallon tender. It was 7ft. 1in. wide while the cab was 8ft. 7in. wide providing an 18in. discrepancy that is illustrated here. After running in at Crewe South shed the engine worked from Camden then Willesden, settling at the latter for a time. The Scottish Region was reached via Abergavenny and Stafford in June 1935 when it began a seven year stay at Carlisle Kingmoor. No. 42740 had residencies at Grangemouth, Hamilton (13 years), Greenock (two spells) and Ardrossan before seeing out its career at Ayr. It was condemned in January 1966 and was transported from Eastfield in April to the West of Scotland Shipbreaking Co., Troon, to be scrapped.

OBAN SIDINGS 55263

These two pictures of LMS 2P 0-4-4T no. 55263 see it reversing onto some wagons in sidings adjacent to the shed at Oban. The line to this area left the former Callander & Oban Railway line just before the station and came into use during 1880. The 'Stranraer' type mechanical coaler seen behind the locomotive was installed after Grouping in a rationalisation of the yard and it had a capacity of 40 tons. This apparatus replaced a manual coaling facility that was formerly located on the west side of the site. Around this time, the shed's 50ft. turntable was replaced by a 60ft. example from Cowans Sheldon; the former had been installed at the start of the 20th century. The introduction of the larger turntable allowed larger locomotives to be based at the shed, such as 4-6-0s, as previously nothing larger than a 4-4-0 could be based at the shed. However, from the mid-1930s the engines allocated to the shed were confined to 0-4-4T, 0-6-0s and 4-4-0T and at Nationalisation five locomotives resided at the shed. Twenty two 0-4-4T found their way to the shed under BR and stayed for varying periods. Eleven 0-6-0s were also at Oban while two 2-6-0s, nos. 46460 and 46468, worked from Oban in the early-1960s.

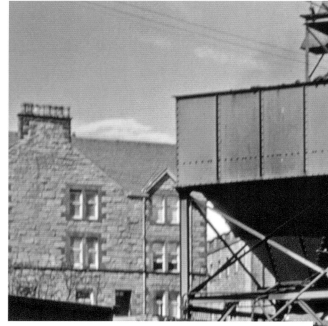

OBAN SIDINGS 45049 ➧

LMS Stanier Class Five 4-6-0 no. 45049 was made by the Vulcan Foundry in October 1934. It began service with a 14 element domeless boiler, no. 8666, which would have been replaced in the late-1930s with a 21 element domeless boiler. In this study of no. 45049 a sloping throatplate boiler is carried, which was fitted from July 1954 until August 1959. August 1956 saw the locomotive's final move to Stirling; it was condemned while there in August 1963. Oban shed was closed during 1962/1963 and a DIY superstore and supermarket currently occupy the location.

PERTH 44931

No. 44931 was built at Crewe Works in April 1946 and was the last engine to be made as part of order no. 460. The engine entered traffic with boiler no. 12441, which had 28 bifurcated elements and top feed on the second ring. A boiler with top feed on the first ring was fitted from July 1951 until the latter half of the 1950s, then it reverted to the previous type; seen here with later pattern top feed. In 1948 the locomotive was allocated to Dalry Road shed, however, by 1950 the engine had reached Perth shed and was in service from there until withdrawn in October 1965.

PERTH SHED 60041 ➡

Gresley A3 no. 60041 *Salmon Trout* was manufactured at Doncaster Works in December 1934 and its first base of operation was Edinburgh Haymarket shed. The engine subsequently only had one other move, which was across the city to St. Margaret's in July 1960 and it worked there until withdrawn in December 1965. The locomotives built in the last batch of A3s were fitted with 'banjo' domes that housed the perforated steam collector and as a result the boiler design was designated diagram 94A. Both types of A3 boiler were interchangeable and the vast majority of the class carried both types during their lifetime. *Salmon Trout* waited until relatively late in its life before changing type and acquiring a domed diagram 94HP boiler in February 1958, which is seen fitted here. This was boiler no. 27003 that had previously been paired with no. 60092 *Fairway*, no. 60089 *Felstead*, no. 60086 *Gainsborough*, no. 60080 *Dick Turpin*, no. 60072 *The White Knight* and no. 60048 *Doncaster* (from new as boiler no. 9573). It would appear that the boiler was last used in no. 60038 *Firdaussi* between September 1959 and June 1961. No. 60041 *Salmon Trout* reverted to using the diagram 94A boiler after no. 27003's removal.

PERTH SHED 45692 ☜

No. 45692 *Cyclops* was erected at Crewe Works in March 1936 with a sloping firebox boiler that had a firebox heating surface of 181.1 sq. ft.; the vertical throatplate boilers had a firebox heating surface of 162.4 sq. ft. The superheater had 21 1¼in. diameter elements that were 11 swg thick and the flues were 5⅛in. diameter giving a total heating surface of 235 sq. ft. The locomotive received a Stanier 4,000 gallon tender with a nine ton coal capacity when new; the type it is pictured with here. Also when new, the engine had the Crimson Lake livery with yellow and black lining applied. Subsequently only the BR green livery was applied and this happened during June 1951. No. 45692 had been present in the Scottish Region from December 1940 when it had been sent on loan to Polmadie from Patricroft shed and the move was made permanent the following month. It left Polmadie in August 1954 for Perth and from the latter it would have worked passenger services to Glasgow, Edinburgh, Aberdeen, Dundee and Carlisle. In *The Jubilee 4-6-0s* (2006), *Cyclops* is noted as being quite a way from Perth on 27 July 1958 when it was spotted at Cleethorpes. Corkerhill became the engine's new home in May 1960 and it left service at the end of December 1962.

PERTH 44900 ☜

In the area south of Perth station, with what appears to be a livestock train, is Stanier Class Five no. 44900 - a Carlisle Kingmoor resident. Approximately 135 of the class were allocated to the shed from 1950 with a number of these lengthy stays. No. 44900 had been the first of seven to be constructed at Crewe Works during October 1945. The engine has been fitted with AWS, the protection plate visible, but this was attached at an unknown date. The first to be fitted was no. 44911 from April 1956 at Doncaster Works. No. 44900 was left service in June 1967.

PERTH SHED 55215 ☚

From this vantage point (which appears to be from the top of a bike shed) the shed yard at Perth has been captured along with CR McIntosh Standard Passenger 0-4-4T no. 55215. Construction was carried out by St Rollox Works in April 1912 and it acquired CR no. 457. From 1948 until withdrawn in October 1961 the engine was allocated to Oban shed and it appears to be at Perth in store. The shed, also known as Perth South, was brought into being by the Scottish Central Railway during the late-1850s. It was situated on the west side of the SCR line from the south; a locomotive works also built by the SCR and in use until the end of the 1920s, was located on the eastern side. The shed, measuring 200ft. by 140ft., was built using stone and had seven roads for stabling engines. As well as a coal stage, a 45ft. turntable was installed, this later becoming 50ft. and finally 70ft. in 1915. During the 1930s the shed building was deemed inadequate by the LMS, who then embarked upon an improvement scheme. A new shed was constructed directly to the south of the old building, with the new structure containing eight through roads and a two track repair shop adjoined the west side. Brick and corrugated steel sheeting was used as the construction materials. BR closed the site in May 1967 and the land has since become occupied by housing, a supermarket and an industrial estate. Note the snow ploughs seen behind the locomotive and the springs seen to the right; no. 55215's dome could be the one seen behind the telegraph pole next to them. Behind the 0-6-0 and 4-4-0 on the repair shop road is the shed for the steam crane.

PERTH 73149

A Standard Class 5 4-6-0 takes on water at Perth shed. No. 73149 was built at Derby in March 1957 with British-Caprotti valve gear, which had been developed on twenty 'Black Fives' built after Nationalisation. At first these locomotives were reported to be slow at setting off from stationary, despite being praised for their running at higher speeds. This led to an alteration of the valve settings that eliminated the problems at low speed and allowing the improved setup to be incorporated on the Standard Class Fives. The British-Caprotti valve gear was also expected to add 10,000-12,000 miles on to the expected time between maintenance of the valve gear and thereby reducing associated costs, but it is unlikely that BR saw this come to fruition. No. 73149's initial allocation was to St Rollox and the next and final move was to Stirling in November 1966, with withdrawal following in December. A curved coal ramp with cover originally served Perth shed and it was located on the west side of the yard. During modernisation at Perth in the late-1930s a LMS No. 1 type mechanical coal plant (seen behind the locomotive to the right) was installed in its place.

PERTH SHED 57264

An early Drummond 'Jumbo' 0-6-0 locomotive is pictured running light between Perth shed and Perth station. The engine was built as part of order no. E580 by Neilson & Co. in December 1884 and was given CR no. 685. The locomotive had the distinction of being rebuilt twice by the CR, with only two others so treated. The engine retains its CR dome, chimney and smokebox door handle, but has lost its outside brake rods. No. 57624 was resident at Stirling from 1948 until withdrawn in September 1961 and it was later scrapped at Inverurie Works. Four companies had converged on Perth during the late-1840s; the Dundee, Perth & Aberdeen Junction Railway, Edinburgh, Perth & Dundee Railway, Scottish Central Railway and Scottish Midland Junction Railway and they all erected sheds in Perth for stabling of their engines. After the amalgamation of these companies with others during the 1850s and 1860s, three companies were left; the Highland Railway, North British Railway and Caledonian Railway.

PERTH 72008

BR Standard Class 6 Pacific no. 72008 *Clan MacLeod* was the penultimate member of the class to be built at Crewe Works in March 1952. The locomotive went to Carlisle Kingmoor to begin its career and it remained there until it was the last of the class to be withdrawn in April 1966. After the Scottish engines had left service in 1962 the remainder were based at Carlisle Kingmoor and were not removed from their duties until 1965. Some of the modifications applied to the class and no. 72008 included; changes to the pony truck lubricators, removal of downs sanding gear, addition of a safety link between engine and tender and LMS-type return crank. *Clan MacLeod* is heading south with an unidentified passenger service and has just passed under the Edinburgh Road bridge.

PERTH 60002

LNER A4 Class Pacific no. 4499 *Pochard* was built at Doncaster Works in April 1938 as works no. 1872. The name lasted less than a year as it was removed in February 1939 when the locomotive returned to Doncaster Works for its first general overhaul. When it returned to traffic in April it carried the name *Sir Murrough Wilson*, albeit covered up for a few days initially, despite no naming ceremony taking place. At this time the opportunity was also taken to fit the locomotive's number in steel cut-outs and 'LNER' on the tender was also applied in this manner; these being in the Gill Sans typeface. The locomotive was based at Gateshead from new until August 1943 when it was transferred to King's Cross. It returned to Gateshead in October and worked from there until withdrawn in May 1964.

PERTH SHED 60097

Seen entering the shed from the north end under the Edinburgh Road bridge is A3 Pacific no. 60097 *Humorist* with large smoke deflectors and a double chimney; the locomotive had a long association with both of these modifications. In April 1929 the engine was constructed at Doncaster Works as LNER no. 2751 and several years later in July 1937 it was the first (and for a considerable time the only) member of the class to be fitted with a double blastpipe and chimney. By January 1938 *Humorist* had acquired wing-type smoke deflectors after smoke drifting problems associated with the double chimney; also at this time the chimney beading was discarded. The large smoke deflectors employed on the Peppercorn classes were an addition in May 1947 replacing the wing-type deflectors and this was followed by reversion to a chimney with beading in June 1948. Subsequently a Peppercorn A1 Class type chimney was used on the locomotive from April 1951. *Humorist* also had a prolonged pairing with its tender with coal rails; a type used by the locomotive from entering traffic. Tender no. 5274 was built for the locomotive, but by August 1929 tender no. 5265, which had originally been paired with LNER no. 2555 *Centenary*, had come into the possession of *Humorist* and remained with it for the duration of its career. The locomotive was allocated to Doncaster, Grantham and King's Cross before arriving in the Scottish Region at Haymarket in July 1950. Apart from a month from January 1954 when allocated to Carlisle Canal shed, the engine was at Haymarket until December 1961. From this time St. Margaret's was its home until being condemned after returning to Doncaster for repair in August 1963.

PERTH SHED 45697

As well as there being a lack of dedicated mixed traffic locomotives in service for the LMS at the time of Stanier's appointment as CME, the shortcomings of the company's passenger locomotives had only partially been addressed with the introduction of the Fowler Royal Scots. A new passenger engine design was prepared for another 4-6-0 like the mixed traffic Class Five, but with 6ft. 9in. diameter driving wheels and three cylinders measuring 17in. diameter by 26in. stroke. The design also featured the taper boiler, axleboxes and low-degree of superheat that Stanier favoured. Fifty-eight were initially ordered from the LMS works at Crewe and Derby in mid-1933 and they were to be built in 1934, but the number subsequently almost doubled when a further 50 were sought from the NBLC in October 1933. Construction continued apace until December 1936 when the last of the class was completed at Crewe Works bringing the total to 191. No. 45697 emerged from Crewe during April 1936 with a sloping throatplate firebox, dome mounted regulator, separate top feed and a 21 element superheater. The latter apparatus had a new element arrangement when fitted to nos. 5696-5701, which increased the heating surface to 268 sq. ft. The locomotive carried the name *Achilles* from entering traffic. After Nationalisation the engine was allocated to Blackpool, Carlisle Kingmoor, Blackpool, Farnley Junction and Leeds Holbeck. Withdrawal came in September 1967.

POLMONT SHED 62691

A locomotive out of action at Polmont shed is this LNER D11/2 Class 4-4-0 no. 62691 *Laird of Balmawhapple*. Construction was carried out by Armstrong Whitworth & Co. Ltd during November 1924; the final seven class members were completed by the company during the month. The only major alteration that was applied to the class concerned the cylinders and valve travel. When built the cylinders had 10in. piston valves with a maximum valve travel of 4⅛in., steam lap of 1in. and max. cut-off was set at 75%. The new cylinders had 8in. piston valves, 5¾in. max. valve travel, steam lap of 1½in. and max. cut-off was increased to 77%. LNER D11/1 no. 5505 *Ypres* was the first to be changed, but further progress was not urgent and the task continued through to the late-1940s; this locomotive, as LNER no. 6398, was altered sometime in the first half of the 1940s. No. 62691 received its name in April 1925, with its valances removed during June 1926. A drop grate was subsequently acquired as was a curved handrail at the front of the smokebox. The locomotive was allocated to Haymarket shed when seen here at Polmont, as was no. 62692 *Allan-Bane* pictured behind. No. 62691 was initially based at Glasgow Eastfield shed but later moved to St. Margaret's in December 1931. In April 1943 the engine began its allocation to Haymarket, where it could work between Glasgow, Arbroath or Dundee heading passenger trains. An irregular working for the class at the shed took them south of the border to Newcastle with a meat train. No. 62692 was withdrawn in November 1959 but no. 62691 was not condemned until November 1961.

POLMONT SHED 62471

D34 4-4-0 no. 62471 *Glen Falloch* was made at Cowlairs Works in October 1913 and was the last of the first five to be built. The engine was originally fitted with a Robinson 22 element superheater, which gave a heating surface of 192.92 sq. ft. The total boiler heating surface was 1346.06 sq. ft. The locomotive spent a significant period of its career based at St. Margaret's shed, which was one of the main stabling points for the D34s. During service for the LNER the main duties for the class at the shed were passenger services that took them to places that included; Dundee, Perth, Hawick and Berwick. The Edinburgh suburban traffic was also worked by the D34s, as could be express goods trains and an assortment of special services. They were relegated to local services by the time BR oversaw their use, but it seems that St. Margaret's could not find a use for no. 62471 at the time of this picture as the engine appears to have been put into storage at Polmont shed; *Glen Falloch* later left service in March 1960. Polmont Junction signal box is seen behind the locomotive.

POLMONT SHED 65342

Polmont shed was erected for the NBR and was ready for use during 1914. The company placed the five road timber building just to the west of Polmont station and close to Polmont Junction on the south side of the line between Edinburgh and Glasgow. The Edinburgh & Glasgow Railway had opened Polmont station on 21 February 1842. The shed was closed during May 1964 and the facilities were removed with the land remaining vacant afterwards. J36 0-6-0 no. 65342 is a 'foreigner' at the shed and was visiting from Bathgate shed, which was its home throughout the BR period. It was withdrawn in February 1960.

ST BOSWELLS SHED 64948

A Gresley J39 0-6-0 appears to have come off the turntable at St Boswells shed. The shed was located at the east side of the station; the 'down' platform waiting room and branch line bay platform can be seen to the left of the stone-built two track shed building. The shed was built by the NBR on 17 June 1850 and was closed by BR during November 1959, but is still in existence as part of commercial premises. No. 64948 emerged from Darlington Works in April 1938 as part of an order for 38 members of the class. Darlington was the main works responsible for constructing the J39s and by the end of 1941, 261 locomotives in the class had been erected there; the remainder of the 289 J39s being the product of Beyer, Peacock & Co. The locomotive had a number of variations when built from the engines that had initially been constructed in 1926. These included; screw reverse, double handle slide regulator, exhaust steam injector and Fountain sight feed lubricator. No. 64948, as LNER no. 1862, was paired with a group standard 4,200 gallon tender throughout its time in service and this also had a coal capacity of 7 tons 10 cwt. Subsequently longer handrails have been attached to the tender at the cab end. Also fitted are removable steam chest covers (seen below the smokebox door), which was a post-1934 modification applied to the class. The locomotive was allocated to Carlisle Canal shed when this photograph was taken and was withdrawn from there in April 1960. The engine had arrived there when new and its sphere of operation would have been north to Dundee, Thornton and Edinburgh as well as eastwards to Newcastle. After Nationalisation local goods were the mainstay of the class at Carlisle Canal, with an occasional passenger service to places in the immediate vicinity possible.

ST BOSWELLS STATION 60093

St Boswells station was opened by the NBR on 20 February 1849, but the name was not exclusively this until 1865 as Newton St Boswells, Newtown Junction and St Boswells Newtown were used up to this date. The station was on the Waverley route and was a meeting point for a number of branch lines including the Kelso and Reston branches. A three storey station house was located on the 'up' platform and it had a booking office, refreshment room, waiting room and stationmaster's accommodation. Covering on the 'down' platform was not provided at first, but it was later acquired, as was the footbridge seen in the distance. The station was closed on 6 January 1969 and the site was cleared in the early-1970s. Gresley A3 Pacific no. 60093 *Coronach* is seen at the 'down' platform. The locomotive was built at Doncaster Works in December 1928 and its first allocation was to Doncaster shed. A brief spell at King's Cross shed occurred in 1930, but another move did not happen until March 1939 when Haymarket became its new home. Almost two years were spent there before *Coronach* made its final transfer to Carlisle Canal shed in January 1941. In December 1958 the engine was equipped with a double blastpipe and chimney, but was one of 22 A3s not to carry smoke deflectors and one of four based on the London Midland Region specifically excluded from having them fitted. As LNER no. 2747 the locomotive had been involved in smoke deflecting experiments in 1931. However, the arrangement was unsuccessful and it returned to standard in the early part of 1933. Withdrawal occurred in April 1962 and it was one of 12 A3s to leave service during the year.

STIRLING SHED 57246

One of the Drummond 'Jumbos' from the first order is seen in front of the south entrance to Stirling shed. The engine was constructed by Neilson & Co. in November 1883 and was initially given CR no. 298, but this subsequently became no. 539. No. 57246 was in service at Stirling from at least 1934 until withdrawn in September 1961. Stirling had eight long-term residents in the 1950s belonging to the class, with a further 12 being based at the shed for shorter periods of time.

STIRLING SHED 55222

On 1 March 1848 Stirling station was opened by the Scottish Central Railway and with it was a timber-built engine shed, which adjoined the end of one of the platforms. It was two years before the SCR added a more permanent building constructed from stone and this contained four roads. The shed was located on the eastern side of the southern approach to the station. In storage at Stirling shed is this CR 439 Class 0-4-4T locomotive no. 55222. The engine was erected at St Rollox Works in August 1914 as CR no. 223. It was in service at Stirling from 1948 until withdrawn by BR in September 1961. Only eight members of the class resided at the shed after 1950 and only three or four were at the shed at any one time.

STIRLING SHED 56343

A member of the CR McIntosh 29 Class is seen moving wagons on track at the north end of Stirling shed. Just before the end of the 19th century the shed facilities were updated with a new track layout, offices, stores, sand kiln and water tank installed. A 50ft. turntable was also bought for the shed and it found a home in the south west corner of the site. A ramped coal stage, out of shot to the left of no. 56343, was a new addition around 1910. The LMS updated the ash disposal facilities and installed some new water pipes and water columns. The only addition under BR was a 70ft. turntable that was donated by Polmadie shed. This locomotive was manufactured at St Rollox Works in April 1911 as CR no. 430 and was withdrawn from Stirling shed during January 1961. Closure of the shed came in June 1966 and the site has since been cleared, but the building behind no. 56343 is still extant.

THORNTON JUNCTION SHED 62677

Thornton Junction was located on the Edinburgh & Northern Railway (later Edinburgh, Perth & Dundee Railway) line between Burntisland and Perth, which opened on 18 July 1848. Thornton station (Thornton Junction from 1850) was operational from 4 September 1848 and the first shed was also in use from this date. The line later came into the possession of the NBR, who upgraded the shed facilities by opening a new four track facility during 1896. It was located close to the junction with the Dunfermline branch (opened 13 December 1849), Leven branch and Methil branch. The shed survived until 1933 when it was closed by the LNER and the buildings were then demolished. LNER D11/2 Class 4-4-0 no. 62677 *Edie Ochiltree* (from June 1925) was constructed by Kitson & Co. in August 1924 and received LNER no. 6384. The boilers fitted to the class were 5ft. 3in. diameter and had a barrel 12ft. 3in. long. The firebox had an outside length of 8ft. 6in. and a grate area of 26.6 sq. ft., with a total heating surface of 155 sq. ft. The boiler worked at 180psi and the tractive effort was 19,644lb. No. 62677 was sent to Haymarket shed for its first allocation and this lasted until April 1957 when transferred to Thornton Junction with two other D11/2 Haymarket residents - nos. 62678 *Luckie Mucklebackit* and 62679 *Lord Glenallen*. From Thornton Junction they were employed on passenger trains to Dundee, Glasgow and Edinburgh. *Edie Ochiltree* was moved to Dunfermline shed in June 1959 but this arrangement lasted only two months as the locomotive was removed from service in August.

✦ THORNTON JUNCTION SHED 68332

Taking on water and receiving oil at Thornton junction shed is a J88 Class 0-6-0T locomotive, no. 68332. Cowlairs completed construction in March 1909 and the engine was the first of six to be erected at the works in March and April of that year. A boiler with dome-mounted safety valves and combination injectors were originally fitted, but when renewal of the boiler was required after Grouping Ross pop safety valves were used and repositioned to the top of the firebox, while the combination injectors were retained. It would appear that a pre-BR boiler is fitted as a flared casing surrounds the safety valves whereas on later boilers this was square. In November 1952 the locomotive had a vacuum ejector fitted in addition to the steam brakes that had been used from new. This was done so it could shunt fitted goods wagons at Markinch where there was a paper mill and whisky bottling plant. No. 68335, also at Thornton Junction, was similarly fitted November 1953. Ten of the class were at the shed from 1950 and nine of them were ultimately withdrawn from Thornton Junction; no. 68335 left service from Dawsholm in October 1962 as one of the final surviving J88s. No. 68332 was condemned to the scrapyard in August 1960.

THORNTON JUNCTION SHED 65910

The LNER placed the new shed on the branch line to Dunfermline and slightly to the west of Thornton Junction. The number of tracks was increased to six and the material chosen for construction was corrugated iron sheeting; a repair shop was also included on the site as were a mechanical coaling plant and 70ft. turntable. Pictured outside the shed is Gresley J38 0-6-0 no. 65910 built at Darlington Works in March 1926. The works took five months to construct the 35 members of the J38 Class, beginning in January 1926. When no. 65910, as LNER no. 1411, entered traffic the engine was equipped with a 4,200 gallon group standard tender, however, this was exchanged in 1931 for a 3,500 gallon-type. The change occurred because the larger tender was required for either an O2, D49 or J39 Class locomotive and all other J38's subsequently had their tenders replaced between 1931 and 1933. A diagram 97 boiler was fitted to this locomotive from May 1950 until it was withdrawn in July 1966. The main difference between the 97A and 97 types was that the tubeplate was repositioned 6in. further forward thus reducing the heating surface in the tubes (912.25 sq. ft. to 871.75 sq. ft.) and superheater (289.60 sq. ft. to 271,80 sq. ft.). The chimney was also repositioned six inches to the rear on the fitting of the diagram 97 boiler. The locomotive was sent to Dundee for its first allocation but moved to Thornton Junction in December 1943. Goods and coal traffic was worked from the shed both in the local area and further afield. The shed ceased to be in use from 1967.

TILLYNAUGHT STATION 78054

After the Great North of Scotland Railway took over the Banff, Portsoy & Strathisla Railway in the late-1860s, the GNSR sought to extend the line from Portsoy to Elgin. This received authorisation in July 1882 and was completed by mid-1886. The line took in places such as; Cullen, Portessie, Portgordon, Garmouth and Calcots before reaching Elgin. Tillynaught station provided a junction between this line and the Banff branch; the station was known as Tillynaught Junction from when it opened on 1 September 1859 to the beginning of the twentieth century. Both of these pictures of no. 78054 show it in charge of the service between Banff and Tillynaught. The locomotive belonged to BR Standard Class Two and it was built at Darlington Works in December 1955 with the first allocation being to Motherwell. Three other members of the class also arrived at the shed and their duties were moving local freight and coal trains. No. 78054 was briefly based at Aberdeen Ferryhill shed in October 1956, but by November had switched to Keith shed. The locomotive was allocated there at the time this picture was taken and when not working the Banff branch, services to Boat of Garten from Craigellachie could be undertaken. The engine moved south to Bathgate shed in June 1964 and a return was made to working coal and freight traffic. The end of no. 78054's career came in December 1965 and it was scrapped by Shipbreaking Industries, Faslane. The locomotive was paired with a BR3 tender, as were the rest of the class. It had a water capacity of 3,000 gallons, four tons of coal could be carried and when full the total weight was 36.85 tons. Tillynaught station closed on 6 May 1968.

TILLYNAUGHT STATION D6147

A Kittybrewster-allocated BR Class 21 diesel-electric locomotive, no. D6147, passes Tillynaught Junction signal box and is heading west on the line to Elgin. The NBLC produced a number of designs for BR's Pilot Scheme, which covered the Type One, Type Two and Type Four requirements. The Class 21 locomotives were built to Type Two specifications and initially ten were ordered, the first being delivered at the end of 1958. Before the first entered traffic, however, two orders totalling 48 were placed by BR and these were scheduled to be in service by 1960. D6147 was completed by the NBLC in May 1960 with a MAN L12V18/21 BS diesel engine, which developed 1,100hp. The main generator was a GEC WT 88A 6-pole unit rated 712kW at 1,500rpm. Four GEC WT 440 traction motors were connected to the main generator and were rated 207hp at 350rpm. Blue Star electro-pneumatic multiple working was also used. The final batch of twenty were all allocated to Aberdeen Kittybrewster and worked all over the country. The other members of the class initially worked in the London area, but after difficulties with the electrical system, exhaust and the engine, all the engines were reallocated to Glasgow Eastfield so the NBLC could solve some of the issues. However, the company did not rectify the problems as it went bankrupt in 1962. Paxman supplied new engines to twenty of the class in the mid-1960s and these became Class 29, but these too proved problematic and the locomotives were withdrawn between 1969 and 1971. The Class 21s left service in 1967 and 1968 with D6147 being sent for scrap in December 1967.

BIBLIOGRAPHY

Baker, Allan C. *The Book of the Coronation Pacifics Mk2*. 2010.

Bolger, Paul. *BR Steam Motive Power Depots – Scottish Region*. 2009.

Buck, Martin and Mark Rawlinson. *Line by Line: The East Coast Main Line King's Cross to Edinburgh*. 2002.

Buck, Martin and Mark Rawlinson. *Line by Line: The Scottish Highland Lines*. 2006.

Clay, John F. *The Stanier Black Fives*. 1974.

Clough, David N. *British Rail Standard Diesels of the 1960s*. 2009.

Cornwell, H.J.C. *The Caledonian Railway 'Jumbos': The 18in x 26in 0-6-0s*. 2011.

Dow, George. *The Story of the West Highland*. 1947.

Fox, Peter. *Locomotives and Coaching Stock 1991*. 1991.

Gammell, C.J. *Scottish Branch Lines*. 1999.

Griffiths, Roger and Paul Smith. *The Directory of British Engine Sheds and Principal Locomotive Servicing Points: 2*. 2000.

Grindlay, Jim. *British Railways Steam Locomotive Allocations 1948-1968: Part Three London Midland and Scottish Regions 40001-58937*. 2008.

Gordon, Hugh. *Great North of Scotland Railway Locomotives*. 2008.

Haresnape, Brian. *Fowler Locomotives: A Pictorial History*. 1997.

Haresnape, Brian. *Stanier Locomotives: A Pictorial History*. 1974.

Hawkins, Chris and George Reeve. *LMS Engine Sheds Volume Five: The Caledonian Railway*. 1987.

Hawkins, Chris, George Reeve and James Stevenson. *LMS Engine Sheds Volume Seven: The Glasgow and South Western Railway*. 1990.

Hoole, Ken. *North Eastern Locomotive Sheds*. 1972.

Hunt, David, Fred James and Bob Essery with John Jennison and David Clarke. *LMS Locomotive Profiles No. 5: The Mixed Traffic Class 5s - Nos. 5000-5224*. 2003.

Hunt, David, Fred James and Bob Essery with John Jennison and David Clarke. *LMS Locomotive Profiles No. 6: The Mixed Traffic Class 5s - Nos. 5225-5499 and 4658-4999*. 2004.

Hunt, David, Fred James, John Jennison and Bob Essery. *LMS Locomotive Profiles No. 7: The Mixed Traffic Class 5s - Caprotti Valve Gear Engines*. 2006.

Jones, Robin. *West Coast: The 175th Anniversary of Britain's Busiest Steam Line*. 2012.

Knox, Harry. *Haymarket Motive Power Depot, Edinburgh: A History of the depot, its Works and Locomotives 1842-2010*. 2011.

Larkin, Edgar. *An Illustrated History of British Railways' Workshops*. 2007.

Locomotives Illustrated No. 103: The LMS 'Royal Scot' 4-6-0s. September/October 1995.

Longworth, Hugh. *British Railways First Generation DMUs*. 2011.

Marshall, Peter. *The Railways of Dundee*. 1996.

Mullay, A.J. *Rail Centres: Edinburgh*. 1991.

Oakley, Michael. *BR Class 26/27 Diesels*. 1981.

Quick, Michael. *Railway Passenger Stations in Great Britain: A Chronology*. 2009.

RCTS. *Locomotives of the LNER: Part 1 Preliminary Survey*. 1963.

RCTS. *Locomotives of the LNER: Part 2A Tender Engines – Classes A1 to A10*. 1978.

RCTS. *Locomotives of the LNER: Part 2B Tender Engines – Classes B1 to B19*. 1975.

RCTS. *Locomotives of the LNER: Part 3A Tender Engines – Classes C1 to C11*. 1979.

RCTS. *Locomotives of the LNER: Part 3B Tender Engines – Classes D1 to 12*. 1980.

RCTS. *Locomotives of the LNER: Part 3C Tender Engines – Classes D13 to D24*. 1981.

RCTS. *Locomotives of the LNER: Part 4 Tender Engines – Classes D25 to E7*. 1968.

RCTS. *Locomotives of the LNER: Part 5 Tender Engines – Classes J1 to J37*. 1984.

RCTS. *Locomotives of the LNER: Part 6A Tender Engines – Classes J38 to K5.* 1982.

RCTS. *Locomotives of the LNER: Part 6B Tender Engines – Classes O1 to P2.* 1991.

RCTS. *Locomotives of the LNER: Part 6C Tender Engines – Classes Q1 to Y10.* 1984.

RCTS. *Locomotives of the LNER: Part 7 Tank Engines – Classes A5 to H2.* 1991.

RCTS. *Locomotives of the LNER: Part 8A Tank Engines – Classes J50 to J70.* 1970.

RCTS. *Locomotives of the LNER: Part 8B Tank Engines – Class J71 to J94.* 1971.

RCTS. *Locomotives of the LNER: Part 9A Tank Engines – Classes L1 to N19.* 1977.

RCTS. *Locomotives of the LNER: Part 9B Tank Engines – Classes Q1 to Z5.* 1977.

RCTS. *British Railways Standard Steam Locomotives Volume 1: Background to Standardisation and the Pacific Classes.* 1994.

RCTS. *British Railways Standard Steam Locomotives Volume 2: The 4-6-0 and 2-6-0 Classes.* 2003.

RCTS. *British Railways Standard Steam Locomotives Volume 3: The Tank Engine Classes.* 2007.

Sixsmith, Ian. *The Book of the Royal Scots.* 2008.

The Railways of Aberdeen: 150 Years of History. 2000

Thomas, John. *The West Highland Railway.* 1976.

Townsin, Ray. *The Jubilee 4-6-0's.* 2006.

Valance, H.A. *The Highland Railway.* 1963.

Walmsley, Tony. *Shed by Shed Part Four: Scottish.* 2011.

Welch, Michael S. *Memories of Steam From Glasgow to Aberdeen.* 2012.

Yeadon, W.B. *Yeadon's Register of LNER Locomotives Volume One: Gresley A1 and A3 Classes.* 2001.

Yeadon, W.B. *Yeadon's Register of LNER Locomotives Volume Two: Gresley A4 and W1 Classes.* 2001.

Yeadon, W.B. *Yeadon's Register of LNER Locomotives Volume Three: Raven, Thompson & Peppercorn Pacifics.* 2001.

Yeadon, W.B. *Yeadon's Register of LNER Locomotives Volume Six: Thompson B1 Class.* 2001.

Yeadon, W.B. *Yeadon's Register of LNER Locomotives Volume Eighteen: Gresley K1 & K2, Thompson K1/1 & Peppercorn K1.* 2000.

Young, John and David Tyreman. *The Hughes and Stanier 2-6-0s.* 2009.

For more information on titles from Great Northern Books

visit *www.greatnorthernbooks.co.uk*

follow us on Twitter: *@gnbooks*